Praise for **YOUR SECOND ACT**

"The timing could not be more perfect for a title like this."

—*Good Morning America*

"Filled with inspirational anecdotes drawn from Heaton's personal experiences (from building her career to love and surviving an empty nest) and the experiences of other people who are pursuing their dreams."

—*People*

"If you've been wanting to start your second act, Patricia Heaton may have just what you need."

—*Today*

"I think it's a really good message . . . think it's more important than ever for people to have that."

—Kelly Clarkson, *The Kelly Clarkson Show*

"After starring in two beloved sitcoms, *Everybody Loves Raymond* and *The Middle*, Patricia Heaton started soul searching for what's next in her life. And she shares what she found in her new book, *Your Second Act* . . . this book is going to be helpful."

—*The View*

"Patricia Heaton wants to help usher people in their 'Second Act.' In fact, the actress has written a book to do just that."

—*USA TODAY*

"I love this because I'm approaching that. I talk about it all the time with my girlfriends. What is our next chapter? What does the back nine look like? . . . I love your back nine right now."

—Kit Hoover, *Access Hollywood*

"It's never too late to try something new. That's what Patricia Heaton will tell you. Heaton's recent experiences spurred her to write *Your Second Act*, a collection of profiles about women, including herself, who have reinvented themselves."

—*Parade*

"There's no wrong way to live your second act. And a new book by Emmy Award–winning actress Patricia Heaton is helping readers set the stage for it. Filled with true accounts of people who transformed themselves midlife—in sometimes-jaw-dropping ways—Heaton hopes readers of *Your Second Act: Inspiring Stories of Reinvention* will not only find motivation but also practical steps to start their own process of discovery. And there's certainly no shortage of inspirational accounts [here]."

—*The Boca Raton Observer*

"A series of encouraging narratives of reinvention . . . each narrative offers a compressed vision of hope and accomplishment that many will find appealing."

—*Kirkus Reviews*

ALSO BY
PATRICIA HEATON

Patricia Heaton's Food for Family and Friends:
100 Favorite Recipes for a Busy, Happy Life

Motherhood and Hollywood:
How to Get a Job Like Mine

Inspiring Stories of Reinvention

Your Second Act

PATRICIA HEATON

SIMON & SCHUSTER PAPERBACKS
New York London Toronto Sydney New Delhi

Simon & Schuster Paperbacks
An Imprint of Simon & Schuster, Inc.
1230 Avenue of the Americas
New York, NY 10020

First Simon & Schuster trade paperback edition May 2021

SIMON & SCHUSTER PAPERBACKS and colophon are registered
trademarks of Simon & Schuster, Inc.

For information about special discounts for bulk purchases,
please contact Simon & Schuster Special Sales at 1-866-506-1949
or business@simonandschuster.com.

The Simon & Schuster Speakers Bureau can bring authors to
your live event. For more information or to book an event, contact
the Simon & Schuster Speakers Bureau at 1-866-248-3049
or visit our website at www.simonspeakers.com.

Interior design by Lewelin Polanco

Manufactured in the United States of America

1 3 5 7 9 10 8 6 4 2

Library of Congress Cataloging-in-Publication Data has been applied for.

ISBN 978-1-9821-4160-8
ISBN 978-1-9821-4161-5 (pbk)
ISBN 978-1-9821-4162-2 (ebook)

*To the brave and adventurous souls
who shared their stories with me in this book,
and to the brave and adventurous souls
who will read these stories and find inspiration
to embrace their own second acts.*

*And to my beautiful family
whom I love above all else—
thank you for your patience and support
through every character change of life!*

CONTENTS

INTRODUCTION

It's 3:00 a.m. and I'm wide awake in a hotel room in Oklahoma City, finishing the final details on the book you are about to read. Why am I in Oklahoma City? I'm asking myself the same question. Technically, I'm location scouting for an upcoming indie project I'm producing. Yes, at my age. I just wrapped the first season of my show *Carol's Second Act* the night before and I'm sick as a dog. I had to skip the wrap party to go home and pack, hop on an early flight, and I've just spent the day fruitlessly searching for a house to shoot the movie in. We're less than three weeks out from principal photography and we still don't have our lead actor. *What on earth was I thinking?*

Timing is everything and it just so happens that the opportunity to independently produce a film didn't come about until now in my sixties. Shouldn't I be relaxing by a pool, hanging out on a golf course, or sitting in a beachside cabana playing canasta with the gals? (I don't know what canasta is but I think ladies in their sixties play it.) It's tempting. But we've had this script for at least ten years and it's now or never—I'm not getting any younger. It's not time to wind down yet, it's time to press on. So on top of my other commitments, here I am throwing myself into the deep end once again—care to join me? I'm embarking on my second act.

All growth comes with a level of pain; I'm feeling it and I'm sure you've felt it at times, too. But somewhere down in the depths of my soul, I must enjoy this. There's a certain excitement in the terror of the unknown. It's kind of what actors thrive on. And so it is with me. I don't feel like I know what I'm doing at this juncture but I'm certainly willing to learn. I'm fortunate to have a team of very talented and dedicated young people around me who somehow just get things done. My challenge is to keep my focus in the right place—not on the result, but on each step in front of me.

The good news: I know I'm not alone in this madness of second act growing pains. There are countless people in the world right now finding drive, purpose, and passionately reinventing themselves in all kinds of beautiful ways. I've found tremendous inspiration from the people you are about to meet in this book. Their strength, commitment, and willingness to step out in faith and desperation—all inspire me in ways I was not expecting when I started this project. I mean, I thought a book about second acts would be a good idea at first and I wanted to inspire others. I just had no idea how much I would be personally impacted through this process.

You see, this book is a by-product of my own personal transition in life. You'll read more about my story in the first few chapters, but as I was setting out on my own second act journey, I wondered about the stories of others and what made them decide to leap into the unchartered territory of reinvention. I thought about all the misconceptions that come with getting older and the questions I had in my own heart—is it too late? Am I too old? Am I too crazy? (Don't answer that.) But beyond the questions in my heart, there were dreams. Dreams and desires I had placed on hold because of whatever pressing thing in the moment that was taking my time—motherhood and family, my career, life. I couldn't let go of those things that were sitting on the sidelines of my heart, I had to bring them to pass. And that is what a second act is all about.

Second acts can be by choice: a new career, an artistic expression, a mentoring opportunity; or they can be due to a change in circumstance: a divorce, the death of a loved one, a layoff, or the empty nest. Second acts can be about self-fulfillment and they can be about service to others. Your second act is your call. It's personal to you. It's your path and your journey.

As I talked to my friends who have already transitioned into their own second acts, and began collecting stories for this project, I realized there is so much to glean from others' experiences. I have personally found new strength and determination as a result. This is my hope for you, too. As you read, don't let yourself become a passive observer. We do that all too often nowadays. Instead, look for yourself in these stories. Find common hopes, dreams, and fears to connect with. Let the strength you read about in these pages become your strength. Let the creativity and resolve connect with the creativity and resolve in your own heart.

My greatest desire for this project is to empower you on the next steps of your journey in this life—to find meaning, purpose, hope, and fulfillment on the adventure that awaits you—the adventure that is *Your Second Act*.

Your Second Act

In the Beginning: My First Act

"Life is either a daring adventure or nothing at all."

—Helen Keller

Bread, booze, and burrata. If anyone would have told me a few years ago that I would be giving up my three most favorite things on the planet (hubs and boys excluded, of course), I would have taken you straight to the nearest psych ward—because that's just pure craziness.

But getting old makes you do crazy things . . . or is it that you've finally become sane, and realized what matters most?

In any case, here I am today, over two years without my gorgeous old fashioned, my caprese salad, or my brioche loaf. Why, you might ask? Well, like with so many other things, I blame it on my kids. I'm sixty-two, and my boys don't seem anywhere near having children, or even steady girlfriends, yet. It could be a good ten to fifteen years before that happens—if it happens. That would put me firmly in my seventies by the time I get to be somebody's "Nana." God forbid I'm a drooling, wrinkled sack of bones propped up in a Rascal, receiving the reluctant but compulsory peck on the cheek from little, frightened grandkids.

So because my body and mind are in decline, I decided I need to do everything in my power to keep death at arm's length and keep myself in tip-top shape, even if it means saying good-bye to Gorgonzola, farewell to French toast, and so long to sauvignon blanc!

Now, no one is guaranteed a single day of life, but assuming I have at least a few years left (God willing) I want to make the most of them.

But there's another reason I wanted to make some changes. The glorious years of raising my family are behind me, and during the time I was deep into them, I didn't have much time for anything else other than acting. Now that the boys have more or less launched, some space has opened up in my life to explore those other interests that were put on hold twenty-some years ago. Now if I could only remember what they were . . . just kidding.

I have lived a life beyond my wildest dreams, and I'm so grateful. Life wasn't handed to me on a silver platter by any stretch. I've worked hard, skinned my knees, cried my eyes out, regretted, doubted, and second-guessed myself along the way. Handing everything over to God changed my life. I've gone up and down many different paths, and looking back, I see how the seed for my second act was clearly planted in my first act. I think you'll find the same is true for you, too.

My first act was, and still is, of course acting, which has been my passion since I can remember. I heard passion described like this: When you do what you love to do at a moderate level, you can call it a hobby. But when you go all out with it to the point that someone deems you one step short of crazy, that's passion.

Throughout the years, I'm sure people looked at my life and thought that I have indeed been one step short of crazy in my pursuit of acting. During my early years in New York, a college roommate visited me in a studio apartment I was renting and I heard that when she went back to Ohio she told everyone, "Patty lives in a shoebox!" She was right. But once you've garnered some success in your career, most people find "crazy" to be perfectly acceptable.

Growing up, I had no encouragement from anyone to pursue acting or to get into the entertainment business. It wasn't that anyone dismissed me or discouraged me, it's just that no one in my family had any connection to that world. However, I've just naturally been a performer all my life. As early on as elementary school I was making up songs in Sister Delrina's class and performing them like I was on Broadway—minus my name in lights and the moldy dressing rooms in the basement. And when my older sisters would bring home a new Barbra Streisand album or the cast recording of *Oliver!* or *The Sound of Music*, I would immediately memorize the songs and have all my girlfriends in the neighborhood learn them, too, so we could sing for family and friends, or at the very least, belt those tunes out into the universe as we sailed along on a swing set.

I was also an avid reader, and when I had a book with a particularly compelling story line, I would gather my playmates, assign them roles, and act the whole thing out. In fact, everything in my world was potential material for a performance. I loved pretending, I loved dressing up. I had a vivid imagination that was fueled by having only three channels on the black-and-white TV growing up. And no internet. (I just reread that last sentence and realized I am very old.) When you have virtually no entertainment, you pretty much have to be the entertainment you seek. And so I was in every respect! I was fortunate to be surrounded by a gaggle of girls on my street who loved singing, dancing, reading, drawing, creating, dressing up, and playacting as much as I did.

As I got older, my love for performing grew even stronger. I was always auditioning for plays and musicals. Strangely enough, when it came time to choose a college and a career, I didn't immediately decide to major in theater. My mother passed away when I was in the seventh grade, and she was the only one to take notice of my performer's personality. She signed me up for ballet and acting classes, but she wasn't there when it came time for me to figure out where to go to college and what to study. And unlike today, there was no tutoring, no SAT prepping, and no college tours. From our neighborhood, everyone pretty much went to the closest state school. My sisters and brother went to Kent State, so it was assumed I would go there, too, no questions asked. But one bad experience there colored my view of the school. When I was in middle school, I went there to visit my oldest sister, Sharon, and she had me watch the Hitchcock thriller *The Birds*. Pretty scary stuff. We also ate pizza and drank Hawaiian Punch, and the combination of all three of those things made me throw up. I could never look at Kent State the same way again. The only other school I had ever visited was Ohio State. And by "visit," I mean I had gone there to watch my high school sweetheart at a wrestling match one time. That was better than nothing, so I became an Ohio State Buckeye, and that's all the thought that went into my higher education.

I next had to decide on my major. No one ever said, "Gee, Patty, you like to sing and be in plays. Do you think you want to be an actor?" And why would they? My father worked as a sportswriter for the *Cleveland Plain Dealer*, and had no interest in theater or music. No one I knew had ever had anything to do with any aspect of the entertainment industry. My older sister Alice seemed to be headed for an acting career, winning a summer acting scholarship and studying theater at Kent State. But when my mother died, Alice came home to take care of me and my younger sister, Fran, and her aspirations were set aside. So the only other theatrical event in the family was the yearly roast for the newspaper my dad sang in (badly) and acted in (worse). In fact, journalism was what we knew best, so it was journalism I picked. My dad assumed that after college I would come home, and he would use his connections to get me a job at the local paper or with one of the TV stations. At that point in my life, I had never even been on a plane, so the idea that I would end up in Hollywood was entirely un-thinkable.

But I was deeply unhappy in college and it wasn't until the middle of my junior year that I realized the depression I had been experiencing since my mother's death wasn't just due to her passing or the lack of counseling I received for it. It was also because I wasn't pursuing my passion. I liked writing but not journalism—I always thought that I was more interesting than the people I had to interview. That's an actor's ego right there, folks! But in my own defense, there wasn't a lot of anything interesting in Columbus in the '70s. I finally decided I was going to pur-sue a career in acting, or at the very least, change my major.

Making the Switch

It took quite a bit of courage to tell my dad that I wanted to change my major to theater. Think Dorothy approaching the great and powerful Oz. Because both my dad and brother were journalists, and I wasn't half bad at writing, majoring in it made sense to my dad. It's just what our family did. So as I prepared my speech in my head, I just knew I was going to get a lot of resistance, and I dreaded the battle. But I dreaded journalism even more. I finally screwed up the courage to tell Dad. Looking back, I'm not sure why I was so trepidatious. Sure, my dad helped me take out the loan for college, but I was the one paying it back, and if I was paying for college myself, it should be my decision, right? I had a good argument in my mind, but still, I guess we all need our parents' approval. I'll never forget sitting across from him in our living room one weekend, nervously wishing I had Toto to cling to. My dad was sitting there in his T-shirt and jogging shorts, legs crossed, reading the newspaper. It was quiet for a moment. I finally just said, "Dad, I want to change my major to theater." He looked up at me, paused for a moment, and said, "That's fine." And that was it. No problemo. I realized later that it wasn't so much that he was "fine" with theater, he just didn't believe that I would actually pursue it after college. I'm sure he was certain that I would come home, and he would get me a job locally, in journalism, as predicted.

I wonder how often people don't pursue their passion because they feel they need to get permission from someone first?

I wonder how often people don't pursue their passion because they feel they need to get permission from someone first? How often do we take the road of what's expected of us even though it's a road we were never meant to travel?

Baby Steps to the Elevator

There's a scene in the 1991 film *What About Bob?* where an accomplished psychiatrist played by Richard Dreyfuss is helping Bob, a man riddled with phobias, played by Bill Murray. In his office, the psychiatrist explains to Bob that he doesn't have to worry about every detail of his life, he only needs to take "baby steps" or set small, reasonable goals, one choice at a time. Bob feels a sense of relief and renewed purpose. He starts with baby steps across the office floor, then baby steps down the hall, then baby steps to the elevator. The doors open, revealing an elevator packed with people. Unfortunately, Bob is claustrophobic. Bob takes a deep breath, coaching himself quietly to take baby steps into the elevator, and as soon as the doors close, we hear Bob completely lose it, screaming at the top of his lungs as the elevator descends. Gotta love Bill Murray.

Though that didn't go well for Bob, the philosophy is a good one. My journey to a long and successful career in Hollywood was just a series of baby steps, the first one being changing my major in college. Ohio State is not known for its theater department, but that was what was available to me in the moment, so I took it—a baby step. That baby step also had a huge impact on my mental well-being. I was a long way from making my living as an actor, but the feeling of knowing I was doing what I loved, and what I believed I was supposed to be doing, helped alleviate some of my depression.

At this point, I was ready to graduate from Ohio State. I did what I had to in order to finish up a BA in theater on time. It consisted of taking a couple of acting classes, some theater history, costume design, play analysis, and being involved in a few productions. I got it done, but it didn't prepare me at all for a career in the theater, or even for one of those Old West shows at Cedar Point amusement park. In this business, the smart way to go about building an acting career is to go to a reputable theater school. You graduate after having done lots of school productions, so when you're out job hunting, you get a hand up from the schools' alumni. If you come from Juilliard or Yale or Carnegie Mellon, there are a lot of successful alumni who will open a door for you.

Plus, all of your classmates are up-and-coming writers and directors who know you and will cast you in their productions in New York. I didn't have any of that at Ohio State.

After I graduated, I really didn't know what I was going to do. So I went back home and got a job as a waitress at a local Cleveland restaurant that had a slight whiff of the mob to it. I was the sorority girl wearing a Peter Pan collar and pearl necklace among hardened old gals with bouffant hairdos and blue eyeshadow. I couldn't get a drink order straight to save my life. On my second day of work, my high school pal Kathy called me and said, "Hey! Let's move to New York!" Without a second thought, I wrote a note and left it at the hostess desk for my boss, saying, "I quit—I'm going to New York." And I never looked back. This wasn't quite a baby step, but I knew it had to be my next step.

Well, first I had to have one more big conversation with my dad. This one wouldn't be as simple as the last one. I announced to him that I was moving to New York and he said, "Oh no, you're gonna stay here and I'll get you a better job." In that moment it dawned on me that I didn't need his permission anymore, and I gently replied, "I'm not asking you, Dad, I'm telling you." He was a bit taken aback, but I remember I detected a slight smile on his face. And he said, "Well, in that case, I'll give you eight hundred dollars. Good luck." And with that, I was off to the Big Apple!

(Side note: Today, I simply could not imagine letting my kids go off to another city without knowing where they were staying, who they were going with, or what kind of job they were getting. I'm not sure which kind of parenting style is better . . . I suspect my dad's is.)

Kathy arrived in New York before I did and got us a fourth-floor walk-up in midtown with no air-conditioning in July. The only other person I knew in New York besides Kathy was my brother Michael, who I saw very little of the first year I was there. As far as getting a career going, I knew nothing. I had no agent, no manager, no headshots, no acting classes, and no real training—just a little bit of raw talent and a whole lot of passion. I didn't know what I was doing. At all. I think the lesson here is that when the steps you are taking only make sense to you, when you go against everyone's better judgment because you simply can't function on this planet otherwise, when your passion pushes you to seek your fortunes in a place you've never been before, then maybe that's really what you *have* to do. Now, if you can do it in a way that makes a bit more sense than the way I did it—like possibly have an actual plan or make some connections first . . . well, that would be good, too. But when you're on your own like I was, you just say a prayer to your guardian angel and head out the door.

I guess you could say I was operating on a wing and a prayer, minus the wing. But I figured if I would just keep moving forward, doors would open that needed to open, and the ones that stayed closed . . . well, I would pound my head against them until I was bruised and bloodied, and then do it some more. It took about fifteen years before doors actually started opening, but I did get little bits of encouragement along the way. And though there were often times when the flame inside of me sputtered, it never completely died out.

What also made it difficult was that everyone I had grown up with was getting married and having children, buying homes, and finding jobs—basically being normal people with normal lives. I was living with two roommates in an apartment in Hell's Kitchen, sleeping on an old crappy futon, next to a dresser I picked up at the Salvation Army. (Incidentally, stripping that dresser and re-staining it was great therapy for me at a time when I couldn't afford a human therapist.) But not only did I not have a career in acting, I didn't have a career in anything. I was either hostessing at various restaurants, running the Xerox machine at *People* magazine, or proofreading in mergers and acquisitions at Morgan Stanley. I would do anything I could to stay afloat. But you know what? I was okay with that. I was poor but mostly happy, pursuing what I loved. At Morgan Stanley I was surrounded by Wall Street types who drove out to their houses in the Hamptons on the weekend, while I toiled away with my little theater company, trying to produce a play. I never felt any envy or jealousy because I was doing what I loved and didn't need a house in the Hamptons or a car to get there. When I got to my happy place—the stage—I actually felt like the richest, most successful gal in the world.

Even now, I think, *What if it hadn't worked out? What if I hadn't become successful? What if I had spent fifteen or twenty years going down this path and I hadn't gotten* Everybody Loves Raymond *or* The Middle *or any of the other shows that led me to where I am now?* All things considered, I think I would still have been happy that I pursued the path that I did. The fact is, it would have *killed* me to do anything else, like work in an office. The few times that I did have an office job, I had an internal time bomb that would go off around the six-month mark. I would start self-sabotaging—show up late, call in sick—I just couldn't do it anymore. I'd end up getting fired or quitting. I much preferred the variety of working in a restaurant or temp job, where every day was different and I would meet new people constantly. As it happens, that's the perfect temperament for someone in the entertainment industry—new scripts, new actors, new shows—it's ever-changing. So even if I hadn't been successful, I still would have been glad I gave it a shot. Thankfully, things started to happen for me, little by little.

The love affair I had with New York started fading at around year eight or nine. I was getting worn down by the fast pace and the rushing around, without much to show for it. I had taken many acting classes, paid for numerous headshots, lived in seven different sublets and one rented apartment over the course of those years, and I didn't feel like I was making much progress. It wasn't all a complete waste of time. I learned so much from my wonderful two years in the Meisner program taught by the extraordinary William Esper. I had produced a couple of plays and received a good review from the *New York Times*. But I had also gotten married and divorced, struggled with depression, and had mounting debt. There was one distinct moment toward the end of my time in New York, when the smell of the urine in the subway finally got to me, and I decided I had done all that I could in that crazy city. Yes, I was ready to give up New York, but not quite ready to give up acting.

I had been to LA once, to participate in some industrial shows. I was hired to sing and dance about the products of companies like Kinny Shoes and Avon. These industrial shows were paid trips out west that introduced me to the big open sky, the sunshine, the happy attitudes of Californians. So, when my current husband, Dave (who was my then boyfriend), told me he was going to LA for work and asked if I could join him with his frequent flyer companion ticket, I said yes! I was excited to leave behind dreary New York City for the bright and sunny City of Angels. I worked out the details in my mind: I had a little extra money coming in from a commercial I had shot, and I had a cousin in LA who I could stay with. I would take the play I produced in New York and produce it in LA and invite casting directors to see it. It was more of a plan than I'd ever had in my life, and it sounded brilliant to me. Baby steps.

I packed my bags (and a huge box of sample shoes I had bought when I was shoe modeling) and told my very patient roommate, Barb, that I may or may not be back . . . and off I went. I arrived in LA only to find out that my cousin had a cat to which I was highly allergic, so he set me up in the back bedroom of his girlfriend's mother's house in West Hollywood. Right after I placed my toothbrush in the bathroom (with no cat hair, thank God), I set about using my commercial money to produce my play.

There was an openness to LA that I never experienced in New York. Whereas the theater community tended to be smaller and more tightly knit and much harder to break into in New York, LA was very different. People were much more laid back, which I attribute to the year-round gorgeous weather and the abundance of beach access. So I produced the play, got a lot of casting people to attend, and started getting auditions for myself, even though I didn't have an agent. I also started attending an arts group at the local Presbyterian church. I found a community of faith and started a new life.

Laying Down the Dream

Letting go of something you love is never easy. Being willing to release a dream, to bury it like a seed, takes faith and trust. Somehow, a farmer trusts the process of planting a seed, and when he lets go of what he has in his hand, he knows he will get a harvest in return. After all, a seed is really just potential. The question is: In our own lives, are we willing to let go and trust the process?

While I was in New York, I was really struggling for work. I felt like I just couldn't get ahead. I would have angry internal conversations with God. I'd say, "Why would You give me this desire and then shut all the doors? Seriously, this isn't funny!"

I got to the point that when I was auditioning, I just couldn't control my nerves because every role meant so much to me. Each opportunity felt like it would make or break me and I just carried a lot of insecurity and frustration about it all. The irony of the situation was that I believed deep down that God created me to be an actor, but I was behaving like it was all up to me to make it happen. I was not willing to let go and trust the process. I was doing it my way and mad at Him for not helping me. It was at this point that acting became more than a passion; it became an obsession—it became the center of my life. Today, people looking from the outside might say, "Well, acting is the center of your life. It's what you do. You are an actor and producer." And yes, I do those things, but they are not the center of my life. Those things don't define me. If it all went away I would still have an identity outside of that because my faith is the center of who I am.

Back when I was living in New York, I hadn't yet made this internal shift. In my mind, if I didn't become a successful actor, I'd have to retreat to a mountain in Tibet and live in monk-like silence with my shame. I carried this pressure and frustration with me to LA. At the time, the Presbyterian church I was attending was organizing a mission trip to an orphanage in Mexico. I decided to go and roped Dave into going with me. We were just there for the weekend doing some repairs on the building and playing with the kids. We laid down some sod that I was sure would never grow, and fixed a sewage line that I hoped would stay fixed. Though none of us spoke Spanish and none of the kids spoke English, we connected in a meaningful, authentic way. I'll never forget their sweet smiles as they shyly held our hands when we threw them a little party. When the weekend was over, I returned to LA, and I noticed something was different inside me. For the first time in forever, I experienced . . . peace. It was an unbelievable peace that I can't even describe. Unbeknown to me, God had really been working on my heart in Mexico. Afterward, I honestly thought, *Well,*

I don't need to be an actor. I could go right back and work as a missionary in that orphanage and be satisfied for the rest of my life. Being raised a devout Catholic, I knew I needed to have a little chat with God about it all. So I knelt down in my cousin's girlfriend's mother's back bedroom that I was renting in West Hollywood and just said, "Lord, I give it all to you. I get it now. Here's the acting. I will stop pursuing it if that's what you want me to do and I'm happy to go back and work in that orphanage." Then something happened that I will never forget. As the words came out, I could almost physically feel a transformation inside of me. It wasn't an easy prayer and it came from the depths of my being. As I prayed, I had a visual in my mind of a rod bending, which to me represented my will and my pride softening as I made the decision to surrender. And then, suddenly, I felt a release. It's hard to describe, but it was a release of the pressure, worry, stress, and burden I was carrying. I immediately felt light and truly free inside. It was like an exchange took place inside me—I gave God control and He gave me rest for my soul.

I wasn't sure what was going to happen next, so then I said to God, "I'm giving this all to you, but right now all I see before me are upcoming auditions. So I'm going to keep pursuing those things as long as they keep coming and if you have another path for me please show me very clearly and I'll go down that road. But I need you to make it very, very clear." And that was my prayer.

After that, I was very different at my auditions. I wasn't as obsessed with getting the job or scared about running back to Cleveland with my tail tucked between my legs. Mostly I was just excited to see what I could do with the material. I wanted to present something wonderful to the producers, casting directors, or whoever else was in the room. I wanted to make them smile and help them find something they didn't even know was there. It was really actually fun when I stopped worrying about whether or not they liked me.

For me, handing everything over to God changed my life. After my prayer, I had so much more joy and confidence and—lo and behold—I started getting work! I felt reconnected to acting in a way that started to elude me while I was in New York. Acting became fun again—which is the way it should be!

A few years later, I landed my career-defining role as Debra Barone on *Everybody Loves Raymond*, which ran for nine seasons on CBS, followed by my role as Frances "Frankie" Heck on the ABC sitcom *The Middle*. And somewhere in the midst of all that, I took on the role of mother, four times over. But through it all, as my relationship with God deepened, so did my desire for charity work. It started with that trip to the orphanage in Mexico and the impact that it had on me. I couldn't forget my desire to do more charity work; I just sort of shelved it while life unfolded.

When you think about your own life, is there something that you've shelved or set aside because of other obligations or priorities? In our younger years, it's easy to pile our plates with pursuits and good intentions. At age thirty, we don't think of sixty as the time to take life by the reins and do all that is in our hearts. At age thirty, we think we have it all figured out and sixty looks like one foot in the grave! But thirty years is a lot of time to learn, accomplish, and reflect—which is what leads most people into their second act—myself included.

2

Life After Bread, Booze, and Burrata: My Second Act

Let today be the day you give up who you've been for who you can become.

—**Hal Elrod**

A lot has happened since I high-tailed it from my sleepy hometown in Ohio, hit the Big Apple, and then bounced right off of it all the way to LA. Marriage, kids, mission trips, television, movies, and more. My first act was a lot like improv. I mostly made it up as I went along. (Please don't tell my kids I had no idea what I was doing as a mother. They made it. I made it. Hubs made it. All good.) But now I have a chance to think through the next act of my life and have a little more control over my script.

I'm excited to say I'm embarking on some new adventures, even though it took a little time to get to the launchpad. Things seem to have fallen into place, but not without some more soul-searching. You see, back in 2017, my series *The Middle* had come to an end, and even though the producers and cast had all agreed that it was time to go, there was a big empty space in my life when we wrapped. For nine years my daily/weekly/yearly schedule was dictated by that show, and my life had a comforting regularity to it. Suddenly, as a recent empty-nester, I found myself living in a quiet house without boys and looking at a calendar without work. Admittedly, I was looking forward to sleeping in instead of being in a makeup trailer at 6:00 a.m. every day.

About that time, hubs and I were off to England for a little R&R, so I signed up for an online screenwriting class at UCLA. Taking on a writing class might seem counterintuitive to R&R, but I'm the kind of person who always needs a project, or I will spend my days and nights watching telly and eating honey mustard pretzel nuggets. Taking the online screenwriting course would give me a deadline to meet each week to add some structure to my day, and because it was an online class, there was enough flex time to also enjoy the sites of London. Check! Check!

Of course, I didn't expect to write the next big Hollywood blockbuster. In fact, I barely got through the class. Writing a screenplay is probably the most difficult aspect of our industry—and yet the most important. If the script isn't good, then nothing else can make the movie or TV show good—not the actors, not the director, not the costumes or the set. I wanted to learn more about screenwriting, to understand how a writer thinks and what the challenges are for them. Through the class, I began to grasp all that a writer is contending with, and though I've always had great respect for that craft, it grew exponentially as I saw firsthand the many aspects of writing a screenplay, all equally important.

I also learned something about myself. I had a very difficult time putting that first line down on the page because I couldn't make a decision on how to begin and I wanted it to be perfect from the very start—which is the kiss of death when it comes to writing. Even though the instructor kept saying, "Just start! Don't worry! You can always rewrite!" I couldn't seem to jump the hurdle of my own perfectionism. And I still haven't to this day. I will be back at it, but in the meantime, Showbiz interrupted.

As it happened, some months later I signed a deal with CBS to executive produce my new show, *Carol's Second Act*. Of course, a lot happened in that "commercial break" between taking the screenwriters course and moving into my role as a producer. But the point is that I kept stepping out in new directions until I found the right next move for me. Producing my own show from scratch has been a whole new adventure, part of my own second act. The challenge of producing a TV series is quite different from acting. For starters, there's no fun wardrobe, hair, or makeup. An actor's whole focus is on character. But as a producer, I'm a part of every detail of the show. Producing involves a constant barrage of scripts to be read, audition tapes to watch, sets and wardrobe to approve, notes and calls for every draft of script for every episode, reviewing edits, making notes on the edits, and making more notes on the re-edits. It's basically death by a thousand decisions.

It wouldn't be so bad if that was all I was doing, but I'm also carrying the show as the main character, so I have tons of lines to memorize on top of it all. (At least I get a heads-up on what my lines will be during the script editing process.) I'm constantly switching hats between character and producer. Needless to say, I've been thoroughly exhausted this season. Poor hubs—he gets to see me for about an hour after work each day, and all I can mumble is, "I have to go to bed" and trudge up the stairs. It's been a stretch for me in many ways and quite demanding. But I've learned so much not only about the process, but about human relations, leadership, and conflict resolution. Phew!

Although I haven't yet written that script I started in England, my experience from that class helped me as a producer reading through the show's story ideas, outlines, and drafts of scripts. It's exciting and tiring and scary and thrilling to see every aspect of each new episode come to life! Exciting and scary and overwhelming are all feelings common to anyone embarking on a new adventure. Not only are those feelings common, but they're important, because they signal that we've stepped outside of our comfort zone. *Challenge, growth, change*—all words that describe a second act.

Exciting and scary and overwhelming
are all feelings common to anyone
embarking on a new adventure. Not only are
those feelings common, but they're important,
because they signal that we've stepped
outside of our comfort zone.

And I'm finding that those words also apply to another new adventure for me as an ambassador for the Christian aid organization World Vision. I'm finally able to be hands-on in humanitarian work, the fulfillment of a desire that was birthed in my heart so many years ago when I first visited that small orphanage. However, now I am in a position to have greater influence and impact than I could have back then. World Vision is the largest nongovernmental humanitarian organization tackling the causes of poverty and injustice. It was founded in 1950, and today it is helping more than 3.5 million children in one hundred countries. While executive producing my television show is new for me, it's still in a familiar setting. My work with World Vision puts me in a completely different environment. Now, I grew up with the example of supporting charitable work all throughout my life. My father was a big worrier about money, but even so, every month as he sat paying bills at the dining room table, I always saw him writing donation checks to various Catholic charities. He set an example of giving, and I continued it in my own life. Once I became a mother and my career took off, giving financially was often the only way I could support others, because my days and nights were filled with family and work obligations. Honestly, I felt kind of guilty about it at times. I really wanted to do more, but I just couldn't add anything else to my plate besides being a full-time mom with a full-time career. One day, when the kids were little, I was listening to a Tim Keller sermon for inspiration. Tim is not only the founder of Redeemer Presbyterian church in New York City and a *New York Times* bestselling author, he's also a personal friend who baptized our eldest son, Sam. When I finished listening to his sermon, I felt so guilty for not doing more that I ended up calling him. I explained how I was feeling, and he said to me, "Patty, there's a season for everything. Right now, this is not your season. Take some time and be grateful for everything that has happened in your life, because a time will come later on for charity work."

That simple conversation changed my whole perspective. It's true: timing is everything. We can't do everything all at once, even though the desire might be there.

As the boys grew and became a bit more independent, I started to have more time to be hands-on with philanthropy. It started when my pediatrician, of all people, invited me and my oldest son, Sam, who was fifteen at the time, to join him on a medical mission trip to Sierra Leone in West Africa. My pediatrician, Dr. Robert Hamilton, would regularly organize these trips, independently gathering medical supplies and assembling a team of medical and lay volunteers to work in the clinics and serve a host church there. He would often invite his clients to go, and I'm so glad we agreed to join him. That was my first introduction to Africa. The poverty there is very real. Hundreds of people walked on foot for days to stand in line for help. Medical supplies are scarce and qualified doctors are few. The hospital beds (if you can call them hospitals) had mismatched sheets that were donated from other countries, old 1970s florals mixed with sheets covered in superheroes. There were unreliable electric sources and all the medical care was provided by volunteers with donated medical supplies. And yet, the people were so grateful and humble.

That trip reignited that fire within me that was lit during my first experience visiting the orphanage in Mexico so many years earlier. In the weeks following, I started looking for an organization that did the same work and more but on a larger scale, and that was also transparent, efficient, and sustainable. That's how I found World Vision.

For the past six years, I've served as a Celebrity Ambassador for World Vision, bringing awareness of the organization to Hollywood and beyond, and raising money for all of their very worthy programs—especially providing clean water to all one hundred countries in which World Vision works.

Being an ambassador for World Vision is very much a "second act" in my life. My first trip with World Vision was to Zambia, and initially I found it all to be a bit overwhelming, particularly because of all the information they sent me about the country, its people and history, and the many problems that World Vision was tackling, not to mention the sheer magnitude of need. I had difficulty with all the names, places, and acronyms for the partner programs. (Of course, to be fair, I also have a problem with my four sons' names and birth dates; hence the need to ditch the aforementioned bread, booze, and burrata.) Lack of clean water is the biggest issue in most of the places I have visited. Without it, many hours of the day are taken up in getting the water to villages, usually transported on foot by women and children. Not only does that not leave time for vital things like education and entrepreneurial opportunities, but the water is usually not safe for drinking and compromises everyone's health. I wanted to use my platform to make others aware of this very fixable problem and other challenges facing our brothers and sisters around the world.

After more trips with World Vision to other countries including Jordan, Uganda, and Rwanda, I started to become familiar with the various cultures and their histories, the different approaches to solving the issues in each place, and the connectivity of us all. Where once no one in my industry had even heard of World Vision, I have now logged numerous appearances for them on *Rachael Ray*, *The Doctors*, and *Dr. Oz*. On one trip, *Entertainment Tonight* came with us to Rwanda and did a two-part series on the experience! I'm truly grateful for all the wonderful people I've come to know and help through World Vision, and for the way they have opened my eyes and heart to hope, possibility, and love.

But enough about me, let's talk about you. There's a reason you picked up this book. I'd like to think it's simply because you like me, but my better judgment tells me that maybe you or someone you love is in a season of transition. Maybe you are exploring options for your second act, or perhaps you are well on your way and you'd like some encouragement and motivation for your journey. You are absolutely in the right place. For starters, even though you will be reading stories of how people transitioned into their second acts, know that yours doesn't have to look like mine or anyone else's. Your second act is personal to you. Second acts can be by choice—a new career, an artistic expression, a mentoring opportunity—or they can be due to a change in circumstance either planned or unexpected: a divorce, the death of a loved one, a layoff, or the empty nest. Second acts can be about self-fulfillment, and they can also be about service to others.

Some second acts are intentional. You've probably heard how Julia Child and Martha Stewart both made career changes in their forties that paid off in huge ways. Julia Child was previously in advertising and media and it wasn't until age forty-nine that she cowrote her first cookbook, *Mastering the Art of French Cooking*, which set her on a path to becoming a multimillionaire celebrity chef. Martha Stewart was forty when she followed in Julia's footsteps, learning how to cook from her recipe books and then wrote her own book, *Entertaining*, and built an entire lifestyle empire from there.

Some second acts are by chance. Donald Fisher owned a hotel renovation business in the 1960s until one day, at the age of forty, he tried to return a pair of Levi's jeans that didn't fit to a local clothing store. Frustrated by the lack of size options, he and his wife, Doris, opened the first Gap retail store, and the entrepreneur built a net worth more than $3 billion.

More recently, you may have heard of Jamie Kern Lima, recognized on *Forbes'* 2019 America's Richest Self-Made Women list. In Jamie's first act, she enjoyed her career as a news anchor. In fact, that's what she thought she would do for the rest of her life. There was only one problem. Jamie has a hereditary skin condition called rosacea, so without makeup, her skin is splotchy and red. She had a terrible time finding any brand of makeup that could stand up under the hot television lights. It would constantly melt off, exposing her embarrassing skin condition. Too often, while in the middle of anchoring the news live, Jamie would hear her producer in her earbud say, "There's something on your face." Trying to maintain her professional composure while feeling extremely embarrassed, she knew there wasn't something on her face. It *was* her face showing through her makeup.

It was a huge problem that she couldn't solve because there was no cure for rosacea, and she couldn't find makeup that would cover it. Some weeks, she would use nearly her entire paycheck trying every brand she could find. She would look at the advertisements of all the perfect, glowing-skinned young women and think, "How am I supposed to know if this will work for me?" Either she would find a product that was so thick it felt like a mask and would crack and break over the course of the day, or it was just too thin to cover her skin. She spent thousands of dollars over time without success.

Finally, Jamie had an "aha moment" when she realized that if this was a problem for her, there must be other women out there who are as frustrated as she was. At the time, she didn't know that nearly 70 percent of women have hyper pigmentation like she had. But she did know, in her heart, she had to tackle this problem. It seemed so much bigger than just her. To make a long story short, she wrote a business plan on her honeymoon flight to South Africa with her husband and when they came back, they both quit their jobs and launched IT Cosmetics out of their living room.

Over the next eight years, IT Cosmetics became the largest beauty brand in the world. In 2016, Jamie and her husband sold IT to L'Oreal for $1.2 billion, the largest acquisition in the one-hundred-year history of the company.

I know, right? Pick your jaw up off the floor and keep reading because there is a lot we can learn from Jamie's story. Jamie's first act was birthed out of passion, but her second act was birthed out of necessity. You'll read more stories in this book where this is the case. Keep in mind that if you have a frustration in your life, it might be part of your purpose. Solving a problem is a great way to kick-start your second act.

Of course, when Jamie and her husband launched the business, they had no idea what they were doing. They just started hustling one step at a time. First, they had to learn about the beauty industry and find a lab to develop the right makeup formulation. It took about a hundred different formulations before they had their first product that actually worked the way Jamie needed it to. It was a huge victory, but that was only the first step. Next they had to take their product to market, but they kept hearing "no" from distributors and retail beauty stores. They were both working a hundred hours per week, and because most of their money went toward research and development, they had to do everything else for as cheaply as possible. For example, Jamie couldn't afford to hire staff, and since her middle name was "Marie," "Marie" got her own email address and was the head of customer service and the head of PR. "Marie" would email beauty editors and pitch the company founder as available for an interview. They didn't have money in their budget to hire a website designer, so Jamie's husband bought the book *HTML for Dummies* and built their first website himself.

Jamie was so excited the first day their website went live. She thought, *Finally, all of this hard work is going to pay off!* But the day ended with no orders. She thought something might be wrong with the website. Then the second day came and went with no orders. She told her husband, "Something isn't working. I think you did it wrong." Then finally, on the third day, she saw an order come through! She started running all over the living room, jumping up and down, screaming and cheering! Her husband interrupted her and said, "That was me. I placed a test order to prove to you that the website isn't broken."

Sometimes you launch things and you don't get the response you were expecting. How do you decide if you should give up or keep going? At the end of the day, you have to go with your heart and with faith because that will get you through.

Every single thing seemed like such a huge struggle for Jamie and her husband, but slowly and surely their business kept progressing. They finally got their first real order through the website, and then another. Eventually, they started getting some steady traction, averaging about two or three orders a day for the first three years, just enough to keep them afloat. "Marie" was emailing beauty editors, and eventually beauty websites started writing articles on the company and talking about their products.

A pivotal moment in the company was when they landed an opportunity with QVC. QVC seemed like a dream, but it didn't all come together smoothly. There was a lot at stake both financially and as a brand. First, they had to make a huge investment in manufacturing to produce the inventory for the show—six thousand units. The agreement was that anything not sold would be returned. Remember, they were averaging two to three orders per day, so this was a massive financial risk for them. Also, they were advised to use models who were very young and had what was considered perfect skin. Jamie wanted to use real women with skin issues for models, but at the time it had never been done before. The experts told her she was crazy. It was a tough decision and she cried and prayed over it a lot. They had one chance and ten minutes. They had to succeed, and Jamie knew she had to go with her gut.

The day of the show, Jamie was full of nerves when the lights came on and the ten-minute clock started counting down. On air, the first thing she did was to wash off her own makeup and reveal her bare skin with rosacea. She used real women of all ages as models and talked with passion about her story and product. Right at the ten-minute mark, the SOLD OUT sign came on, and when the segment closed, she started crying. Her husband came running out and hugged her, saying, "We're not going bankrupt!"

IT Cosmetics became the largest beauty brand in QVC history and it still is today. They expanded into all major retail outlets and dominated the US market, and when it became time to go global, that's when discussions started with L'Oreal. As part of the acquisition in 2016, Jamie was brought on as the first female CEO of a brand in the company's history.

Fueled by the simple notion that all women deserve to feel beautiful, IT Cosmetics was the first cosmetic brand to use real women with imperfect skin as models and it paid off in a huge way. Jamie is one of a handful of women who can say they've built a billion-dollar company from scratch. She will be the first to tell you that when you are doing something innovative or novel, don't expect the "experts" to be supportive. You have to go with your gut even when it feels like you are totally winging it. It is all part of the process.

Though it's true that second acts can be about taking chances, or taking second chances, the reality is that a change in life isn't about waking

up one day and completely reinventing yourself, or striking it rich, unless that's what you *want* to do, of course. Oftentimes, the changes are
subtle, and one day you look back and realize how far you've come.

While Jamie's story is quite remarkable, you don't have to start with
anything earth-shattering. My sister Alice is now a volunteer at a Boys
& Girls Club in Arkansas, after raising three children as a full-time mom.
My former coworker A.J. is a full-time executive but got training as a
counselor to man the phones once a month at the Trevor Project. Sometimes a second act means taking a step back before you can launch forward. My friend Brent is a fashion stylist who has worked with some
of the biggest talent in the entertainment industry. Enjoying success
at the top of his field, he found that he wanted to do something more
meaningful with his life. He decided to pursue a degree in psychology
and took a job in retail while going to school. It will be four years before
he is licensed but he is willing to put in the time to get to his second act.

A second act can also be about an internal shift or transformation.
Lucy lives in Hershey, Pennsylvania, and when she turned sixty, she decided she wanted to do something special. She searched online for ideas
and unique ways to honor the milestone and saw that someone online
performed sixty random acts of kindness in their sixtieth year. Lucy
liked that idea and decided to do the same thing. She kept a log on her
computer, tracking each act. Every day she updated it and made a note
of where she was, who she talked to, and what she did. It started out as
little compliments to complete strangers: "Your hair looks great today"
or "I really like your shirt." She looked for ways to make people smile
and brighten their day. As a result, she enjoyed delightful conversations
and got to know people she would have never spoken with otherwise.
She would also go online and do the same thing. She would even pay for
someone's gas or give money if she saw someone in need. At the end of
the year, she was overjoyed to discover she had logged over six hundred
random acts of kindness. She plans to do more every single year.

Lucy didn't start a new celebrity career or build a billion-dollar
empire or launch a global franchise chain, but she made an impact.
She added value to the people around her and increased her circle of
influence. Most important, she found fulfillment in doing something

for other people and found purpose that will carry her in the second half of her life.

What if we all focused on ways to improve the lives of the people around us the way Lucy did? It really didn't cost her money. She didn't have to radically change her lifestyle. She simply had to be open and willing to grow and to get out of her comfort zone.

I believe that one of the keys to really finding fulfillment is being open. Open to trying new things, open to learning new things, open to new people, open to new ideas, and open to discovering new things about yourself. And then, being proactive. Take action on those discoveries and keep growing in ways that bring meaning to you, and those around you.

There's no wrong way to live out your second act, and the purpose of this book is to give you some inspiration, motivation, and tools to help you set the stage. Maybe you don't have a clue about what you want the next forty or fifty years to look like. You're not the only one. Maybe you have somewhat of an idea, but you don't really have a plan. That's okay. In fact, you'll see that most of the people in this book accomplished what they did by simply taking one step at a time. My hope is that by the time you finish this book, some of these stories will fuel your resolve, drive, and enthusiasm.

I think this popular quote from *The Curious Case of Benjamin Button* sums it up perfectly:

For what it's worth, it's never too late or . . .
too early to be whoever you want to be.
There's no time limit. Start whenever you want.
You can change or stay the same.
There are no rules to this thing.
You can make the best or the worst of it.
I hope you make the best of it.
I hope you see things that startle you.
I hope you feel things you never felt before.
I hope you meet people with a different point of view.
I hope you live a life you're proud of.

And if you find that you're not, I hope you have the strength to start all over again.

In every stage of life there are common passages, and it's important to learn from people who have gone before you. In times of transition and uncertainty, it's easy to second-guess yourself or start feeling like you're wandering around in the dark. Too often we can get stuck simply because we think we are alone in what we feel or what we are experiencing. But we aren't. You aren't. I promise. We may not all have the same experiences, but we all have the same emotional pool to draw from. We've all felt scared, lonely, sad, uncertain, and frustrated at some point in life. We've also all felt the satisfaction of stepping out into something new and growing as a result. So we can learn a lot from people even if they come from completely different backgrounds and have lived completely different experiences. As you read, you're going to meet some of my longtime friends who've inspired me along the way, as well as new friends who are just like you and me—men and women from all walks of life finding meaning and fulfillment for the second half of life. These are people who didn't have all the answers when they started. They walked through heartache and disappointment. They overcame loss and rejection, and they second-guessed themselves along the way. But they also launched wildly successful businesses and nonprofits, solved issues in the special-needs community, saved thousands of lives playing golf, and set out to solve the global health care crisis, and so much more.

I hope that as you read these pages, you see yourself in the stories and glean wisdom and strength for your personal journey, whether your second act is about changing careers or changing the world. It's time to take a step in the direction of that dream you've been nurturing. It's time for *Your Second Act*.

Life Is What You Bake It

The Second Act Story of Liz Smothers

Liz Smothers is . . . sweet as pie! Owner and founder of the Julian Pie Company, whose apple pies are touted by the Food Network as one of the best foods to eat in all of California, Liz was a stay-at-home mother of five when she decided to get a job to help with the family finances.

Here is Liz's second act story.

I did everything wrong.

At least that's how I felt a lot of times over the years. I wasn't looking to build a pie business and had no idea what I was doing when I started out. I certainly didn't expect to stay in business over thirty years and expand to distribution in 135 stores with national recognition. There were many days I didn't really know what was happening next. I often felt like I had to just put on my football helmet, so to speak, and go for it!

I was born and raised in Kansas and graduated high school in

1955. In 1956, I married my high school sweetheart. It was my dream to be a wife and mother. My husband started out working for the railroad. His first job was in Montana, so off we went to start our life and family together. He worked many years on the railroad and then decided to go to college to get his teaching degree so he could be home more with the kids and me. After our fifth child was born, a friend of his strongly urged him to drop everything and become a full-time preacher at a church he knew of in the South. So we picked up and moved to Alabama. After about five years, he became as anxious to get out of the state as he was to get in. We discussed where to go next, and I said I always loved the West Coast. My husband had a school mate who was the president of the Western Region of AT&T. He reached out to his friend, who offered him a job in California. We didn't have much money, but we had enough to buy the old church bus, and so we loaded up everything we owned and headed west. We ended up in the quaint town of Julian, located just north of San Diego in the beautiful Cuyamaca Mountains, known for its agriculture—and particularly its apples. When we arrived, we were flat broke, but we managed to find a little house to rent on the top of a steep hill. That old bus was so run-down that we would hope and pray it would make it up the hill and then stop once we got there. And sometimes it didn't. We sold that old bus as quickly as we could once we got there and purchased a car to get us around town.

My husband started his new job right away, but I knew I would have to go to work to help make ends meet. After all, we had seven mouths to feed. I answered an ad in the paper for a position at a small bakery in town that was owned by a blind couple. The man was completely blind, and the woman was legally blind, so she had some sight, but she could no longer manage the bakery. I didn't have any work experience at all, but I told them I baked with my mother growing up. They said, "No problem. We will teach you everything you need to know." And they did. Both of them being blind, they explained to me everything about the store and then left me there to run it all by myself. It was up to me to bake, clean, serve, and sell. I gave my whole heart to the task and started by scrubbing the place from top to bottom. I made curtains for the windows and treated that little shop as if it were my own. In fact, people started thinking it was my shop because I invested so much heart into it. At the end of each day, I would take the money out of the cash register and put it into a small coffee can and drive it to the owners' home in the country. I would stay and make them dinner and help them with whatever they might need at the time.

After a couple of years, a BBQ place opened on the other end of town. They offered me an extra dollar an hour to go work for them baking their pies and biscuits. An extra dollar an hour at that time was substantial—an offer I couldn't refuse. I went back to my bosses and asked if they would be willing to match the offer to keep me, especially since I was doing every single job in the pie shop. They declined and opted to hire someone else, so I left and started working at the BBQ restaurant.

After some time working at the BBQ restaurant, the owner of another place in town asked me to come work for them and they offered me another pay raise. This place was right in the middle of town and highly visible. It was also busier than any place I had worked before. There were windows to the street where people could look in and see me making pies.

By this time, I was developing a following of people who would come to wherever I was and buy whatever I would bake. I baked by a simple principle: *You never make your best pie, because the next one will be even better.*

One day, a man came in from Costco and pulled me aside and told me he wanted to buy the pies I was making and sell them in his store. I said, "Thank you so much, but I just work here. I don't own the business." He said, "That's okay. I want to buy *your* pies." I was a bit surprised and not sure what to say. He gave me his card and asked me to think about it. I was flattered by the offer, and it planted a seed in me. I started thinking . . . I knew every recipe by heart for every place I ever worked. I never shared those recipes with anyone; however, I knew my mother's apple pie recipe was better than any other recipe I ever made. I started thinking about what it would be like to make and sell my own pies, making them the way my mother taught me.

You see, I was the youngest of eight children, so I got to spend a lot more time with my mother in the kitchen than some of my other siblings did. When I was just four or five years old, she would let me step up on a box in the kitchen while she was baking. She would give me the leftover scraps from her pie crusts, which I would roll out and cut into a tart using a Mason jar lid. I would then place a slice of apple in the center and fold it over to make my own mini apple tart. Those memories are still fresh in my mind today, and that little nudge from my mother in the kitchen so early on is what fueled me to be where I am.

After the visit from the man from Costco that day, I went home and started to talk to my neighbor about it all. She happened to have a sister who worked to help people set up small businesses, so it got me to thinking more seriously about my next steps. Not only that, her husband was a contractor and builder. By this time, I was fifty years old, and it seemed to be the right time to finally open my own pie shop.

My husband wasn't so thrilled about the idea at first. He was still working for AT&T and had the opportunity for a promotion in LA. He didn't want to let go of the security we had, plus he thought for sure I was going to bankrupt us. But I never gave it a thought that I might fail. I was so confident that my pie recipe was better than anyone else's that it never came into my mind that it wouldn't work.

My husband finally came around, and in 1986 we found a little house on the edge of town and turned it into that first pie shop. Because I had developed a following over the years, my business started with a bang. We were constantly busy from the day we opened and immediately became profitable. The whole family helped out back then, too. My youngest two were in sixth grade and seventh grade. They laugh now because I paid them a nickel or a dime for each pie crust they rolled after school. The kids would roll the dough and my husband would take the "dough" to the bank. We used to tease and call him Ol' King Cole. It probably goes without saying—he retired early.

It wasn't long after the store opened that people started asking about wholesale and where they could find our pies to share with friends and family, so we considered expanding.

We had to learn the wholesale business step-by-step by ourselves.

We didn't know anyone who had done it before, so there was no one to ask. I started out by approaching Harvest Ranch Markets, a local gourmet grocer. I baked three or four pies and took them over to the manager and gave him my sales pitch. He said, "We already have Julian Pies." He had been ordering from another pie maker in the area. I looked at the box of my pies and looked at him and said, "Well, we made these special just for you." He took the pies to be polite. The very next day he called me and placed an order, and we never had to try to sell another pie after that. Store after store wanted them because people were asking for them by name. We now have more than 130 stores we deliver to in San Diego three times a week. We are at Albertsons, Stater Bros., Aldi, and many others. One day, we even heard Dr. Laura Schlessinger bragging about our pies on air during her national radio show. She's a regular customer now and a good friend. Her favorite pie is the Natural made with Golden Delicious apples and sharp cheddar cheese. She is a wonderful patron, and it was always fun to hear that she was trying different pies and talking about them on her show!

It's amazing to think what has happened since that first pie so long ago. I'm not involved as much as I used to be in the day-to-day operations. My sons have taken over the business at this point and my youngest is the CEO. Now, during certain seasons of the year, you can hardly get into our shop. We've maintained our quality and consistency even as we've grown. And if you think our apple pie is good today, wait until you taste it tomorrow.

{ Q & A }

What advice would you give to someone who is exploring their own second act?

First of all, pick one thing and do it well.

At one point, as we were growing, we tried to open an apple farm. Well, we did it, actually. Apples grow great at this altitude, which is why so many people grow them here. We used the apples for our pies, and we also tried to get into the cider business. It was a lot of work and I was approaching seventy years old. It just became too much to manage, so we sold the farm with the understanding that we would still buy apples from the new owners to make our pies. We were just spread too thin trying to run both businesses. There is a lot that goes into doing a pie right, and so we decided to keep our focus on the pies.

The other thing I would say is, whatever that one thing you do choose is, make sure it's something the heart desires. There are many long days up ahead on whatever road you take. If someone on your team doesn't get something done, you have to take responsibility to fill in the gaps. Make sure you are really passionate about whatever it is you are pursuing, or you won't feel like doing it when the times get tough.

Did you ever feel like giving up?

I never had a thought of quitting. My mother had a strong work ethic, so she instilled that in me. Owning my own pie company is the neatest thing I've ever done in my life. I have always loved making pies and I still do.

It wasn't easy by any stretch. All along the way it seemed like every time I made a turn, I did the wrong thing. It was a lot to learn every part of the process, from how to pick the very best fruit to how to scale your pie crust recipe to fit the growing demand. I started out making the crusts by hand, of course, but as we grew, that wouldn't work anymore. We got a new machine for mass production, and the crust recipe came out completely different. Even though it was the same ratio of "stuff" per pie, it just reacts differently in bulk batches, so I had to tweak the process to make it all work out. There's no pie making school anywhere to show you how to do this. So it was a lot of trial and error all along the way. But you just do what you have to do. Nobody is going to do it if you don't.

Other than the first couple you worked for at the bakery, did you have any other business mentors?

When I first went into business for myself, my team and I went to LA to In-N-Out Burger. They had the friendliest people at the counter so we asked if we could learn from them. They gave us one day to train with their team under one condition. They said, "We will tell you everything you want to know, but you can't write anything down." So we studied their business and followed their model for service and our team is pretty awesome.

One day, some people from Jack in the Box came to our pie shop, and they used our employees as an example of how to work hard, so that was a huge compliment.

What do you think makes your pies stand out from all the rest?

Well, the ability to know how to make a good pie came from my mother, of course. She was a little-of-this-and-a-little-of-that kind of person. I knew the pies had to taste a certain way, so I would tweak my own recipes until they were right. So I attribute the quality and taste of the pies to what my mother taught me, and I attribute the success of the business to our employees. We have a wonderful, faithful, hardworking team. Anytime someone comes to work for us, no matter what their job is, they have to learn every single part of the process. They have to know how to select fruit and how to roll a crust. They have to understand how their role affects every part of the process. This helps us maintain consistency with our products, too.

I think another reason our pies are so good is because I would always roll my sleeves up and work with the employees. At first, most of them didn't realize I was the boss because I was working right alongside them. But I found that being present helps to keep the standard and consistency of our pies.

In all honesty, our employees are like a great big family. Early on, I had a young Spanish girl come work for me. She was around seventeen when she started working for us almost seventeen years ago. We've walked through many stages of life with her, getting married and starting a family. She was my sidekick as we grew the business and she is like family to me.

We also celebrate our employees and say thank you often. For example, our bakers arrive very early each day. Once a week we do a big breakfast for them to show our appreciation for their dedication.

What was the reaction from the rest of your family and friends when you started your business later in life, and how did that affect your decisions?

I actually remember being shocked about how many of my friends and family members were so encouraging to me. It was almost like I couldn't let them down. Their faith in me fueled me.

I enjoyed doing the business with my kids. My younger kids are still involved in the business, but my two older daughters had already moved out by the time I got started.

Also, my sister Mary Ann was one of my biggest supporters. She encouraged me all along the way and I leaned on her strength. I'm so grateful we had such a wonderful relationship.

Do you feel like you ever went through a period of "midlife crisis"? What did that look like and how did you resolve it?

Right before I got into business for myself, after my conversation with the man from Costco who said, "I want your pie," I had this fire inside of me and I just thought, I can do this. *It was more of a sense of urgency than a "crisis" per se, but I knew it was a "now or never" situation. I just forged forward and never looked back. I took each problem as it came along and made it one step at a time. I think that moving forward probably saved me from a crisis.*

What would you tell your younger self now?

I would tell myself to not be quite so hard on myself. I would loosen up a little bit and have more fun and just enjoy everything more. I always had this attitude when I was younger that if it couldn't be done my way, I would just do it myself. Well, I couldn't have done it all myself. But I really did strive to make sure everything was just right. Now my son runs the company, and they tease and say he is fussier than I am. Well, I wonder where he got that from?

Did you think about your age or give it consideration?

When I first went into business, we took pictures and we took them from time to time over the years. It wasn't like nowadays where we always have a camera in hand. From time to time, I would look back on the pictures and say, "Oh, look how young I look!"

About every ten years or so I would notice that I was looking different, but I don't guess it ever really bothered me. When I get up and put my makeup on each day, I am right back in the '50s.

What's the vision for your future now?

Well, I'm not techy at all. I feel like I've taken the business as far as I could take it myself. I've had to take a step back and slow down a little due to some health issues, and it was really difficult to let go of the reins at first. But everyone stepped right in to make the transition smooth. The kids are techy, and I'm amazed at how my younger son keeps things up-to-date and operates the business in a way that makes everyone comfortable. He bridges the old way with the new way very well, and I'm so pleased. I feel God has blessed me beyond what I ever dreamed of.

PATTY's POINTS

● **Never underestimate the power of a good work ethic.**

At the risk of sounding cliché, Liz's story screams, "Hard work pays off." And it's true. It was something modeled for her and something she modeled and instilled into her own family. It really is what brought her to the level of success she enjoys today. I love that Liz's story combines the impetus of necessity with a family tradition. Liz was thrown into the deep end at that first pie shop she worked at, and she took up the challenge with gusto—not out of passion, but out of the need for extra income. Because of that need, she worked as if her life depended on it and put everything into that pie shop, treating it as if she owned it. It strikes me that that might be one of the reasons she ended up owning her own shop—from the beginning, she treated every pie shop as if it were her own. She was unconsciously preparing herself for her personal success.

Because Liz included her family on the journey, she has given them an education that they couldn't have gotten in school. She modeled a good work ethic for her kids. What a priceless gift. I'll bet one of the biggest joys for Liz is seeing her kids flourish in the legacy she created.

● **Pursue what sparks joy.**

How serendipitous that Liz's favorite childhood memory, baking with her mother, became the subject of her success. If you are thinking about a second act but not sure what it might look like, perhaps a look back to your childhood might give you an idea. Too often, at this stage of life, many people have slipped into autopilot, so to speak, checking off to-do lists and rushing from one commitment to another. Now is the time to slow down and take time to consider what's in your heart. What was it that used to capture your imagination when you were young? What sparked joy? What gave you pleasure? These memories could be clues to what your second act might look like! Maybe you have to go backward before you go forward . . .

Learn from what doesn't work out.

Like many of the stories in this book, Liz's journey was quite circuitous. She went from one pie shop to the next, and once she founded her own business, there were still more false starts. But with each detour, she learned invaluable lessons about running a business, overcoming setbacks, and bringing the family on board. So maybe those events aren't setbacks after all, but really important phases of the journey that set her up for success in the next phase of her business.

Liz wasn't afraid to move forward, but she also wasn't afraid to step back when things didn't work out—for example, her apple orchard and cider business. These expansions ultimately strained both Liz and the business, so she made the decision to move on. Trying something new that ultimately doesn't work out is just another part of our life education, if we let it be.

You don't have to have it all figured out before you start.

Just because something doesn't work out for you doesn't mean you are doing the wrong thing. It may mean that you just need to do something differently, or like Liz, stay focused on what you do best. Don't let failure define you, and don't let fear stop you from trying again when things don't turn out the way you originally expected. Keep moving forward one step at a time, because you might be surprised at where you end up!

Liz didn't start out with a twenty-year trajectory to becoming the greatest pie maker in the country. She didn't have her career planned out, and oftentimes, she didn't have a clue about what was coming next. She was open to new opportunities as they came. She wasn't afraid of a challenge, and she wasn't afraid to step back when something didn't work out. Liz had a very flexible attitude when it came to her path in life, and she was able to adjust as it progressed.

If you are sitting there today and you don't have your next step figured out, you might be in a better position than you think. Sometimes if we believe we have it all figured out, or if we become determined to do something in a certain way, we can close ourselves off to opportunities that can take us further in life than our original plan. Imagine if Liz had set her sights on taking over that first pie shop for the blind couple. She could have stayed where she was, working for less than she was worth, and hoping one day to have a shot at ownership. Perhaps eventually she would have taken it over, but she would have missed a lot of other opportunities. But because Liz was willing to step out and go where she was valued more, she paved the way for greater success than she ever imagined.

REFLECTION QUESTIONS

1. Where do you see yourself in this story? What part of Liz's personality, character traits, or journey can you relate to or identify with?

    _____

    _____

    _____

2. What is your greatest takeaway from this story?

    _____

    _____

3. Write down five things that spark joy for you, anything from a delicious slice of pie to a perfect pop song, or a possible activity that could be the start of your second act.

    _____

    _____

    _____

    _____

    _____

Nursing the Dream

The Second Act Story of Lisa Johnson

Lisa Johnson knew there was more to life than just working hard in order to retire. As a single mother of four, one of them with special needs, her career as a nurse working the night shift wasn't fulfilling, nor was it supporting the lifestyle she desired for her family. While the income was stable, the schedule was grueling—and finding a reliable babysitter was extremely difficult. One day, she felt inspired to start her own business. It almost seemed crazy at first, since no one in her family had ever owned a business before . . . or even talked about owning a business. But deep down, she knew she had to try. It wasn't easy, but nothing ever was for Lisa. Even during the difficult times, Lisa kept moving forward one step at a time, and that's how she launched her medical staffing company. This year, her company is on track to net $30 million.

Here is Lisa's second act story.

I had every odd stacked against me growing up.

We were an average, middle-class family. My dad was one of the first black officers in the Marine Corps. He always worked hard and expected his family to work hard, too.

I remember segregation and discrimination. I remember my parents trying to shield me and my sister from it. At times, I wasn't really sure where I fit in this world. I wasn't like the other kids at school. In high school, my reading and writing skills were several grade levels behind because I had an undiagnosed learning disability. I wasn't a high achiever like my dad expected. My parents would compare me to my sister all the time, and I didn't think I could ever be enough for any of them. At age fifteen, I started skipping school and running away. I thought school just wasn't my thing. I was always getting into trouble anyway, so why go? Some mornings, I would walk outside to catch the bus and then sneak around behind the house when no one was looking. I'd wait until my parents left for work, then I'd go back inside and watch TV. Or I'd just go to my friend's house.

Eventually, and by a sheer miracle, I got my "D"-ploma, passing high school with straight D's. My dad told me I had the choice to either go get a job or go to college. God only knows why, but I chose college—and then subsequently flunked out.

I was so desperate; I didn't know what I was going to do with my life. I knew I wanted to make a lot of money, but I wasn't sure how, so I joined the military. Logical next step, right? I spent four years on active duty and served in Desert Storm. War will grow you up fast, and that's what I needed to do. Something changed in me during that time, and when I came home, I was different. I went into the Reserves and decided I would pursue nursing school.

I had a strong sense of resolve at this point, and I was determined to get my nursing certification. School had always been a struggle, and this time was no different. I would have to study for weeks to pass a test, when my classmates wouldn't have to study at all. I worked harder than I ever have my entire life and managed to get straight A's.

I enjoyed my career as a nurse and found the highest pay was working the night shift. But four kids and two divorces later, life was just hard. On top of that, my youngest was diagnosed with autism, something you can never be prepared for. I relied heavily on my faith to get me through many difficult days during this season of my life.

Several of my coworkers were also single moms, so we had a good support group between us. My biggest struggle was that I was always running late for my shift because I had to wait for the babysitter to arrive and she was always late. I was supposed to be to work at 3:00 p.m. and sometimes she couldn't even come until 4:00 p.m. My coworkers would try to cover for me, but because I had been severely late a few times, my boss put his foot down. He wasn't going to give me any more leeway, so I had to get to work on time or risk losing my job. I didn't have any other options for child care, so some days I would take the kids with me to work and sneak them into the employee break room until the babysitter could come and pick them up. One day, my boss was there, and I couldn't sneak them in, so I had to just leave them in the car with some books and watch them through the window. They were older and the weather was good. I hated doing it, but I had no other choice. I couldn't risk losing my job. Where would that leave us? My coworkers understood the struggle, so they would watch out the window for me while they were at the nurses' station so I could do my rounds.

It finally got to the point where I knew this setup just wasn't going to work for me or my family anymore. I had to do something different. Around this time, I began to attend inspirational conferences and listen to faith-based inspirational teachings on tape, which greatly impacted the way I saw myself and my abilities. I started to see that I was made for more and there was more for me in this life. When I started to see myself differently, and when I started to understand my potential, I started to see the world around me differently. I had been looked down on almost my entire life, and I finally realized my true worth and value. I knew there was more for me in life, and it was time to start pursuing it.

The nursing home where I worked used large agencies to hire temp staff. I was curious about how all of that worked, and when I looked into it, I learned these agencies were making millions of dollars. A staffing agency contracts with a medical facility to provide medical staff. The facility pays the agency and the agency then pays each staff person directly. The medical facility benefits because they don't have the huge costs associated with managing personnel. The staffing agency makes a profit by sheer volume. The medical professionals benefit because they don't have to apply for jobs all over the place; the agency knows where the job openings are. I thought, *I can do that. I can schedule nurses and send them out for shift work.*

Each day after that, I would wake up and take a step toward opening my own business in medical staffing. I was still working my job as a nurse so it was so exhausting at first. I pushed myself and worked long hours, but I could see the vision of what was possible. I started by forming my corporation, getting licensed, drafting contracts, and on and on. I really did not know my next step until I finished the step that I was on. It was a one-day-at-a-time process.

The day came when I was finally ready to take my first corporate client. I called a nursing home in the area and made an appointment with the manager to discuss my staffing services. The day of the appointment I was dressed to impress! I put on my best skirt suit and did my hair and makeup perfectly. I was nervous and excited and prayed for strength as I walked in. I walked up to the receptionist's desk and handed her my card. She said, "Oh, hi. Our manager is expecting you." A few minutes later, the man I spoke with on the phone came out. I smiled and recapped our conversation as I handed him my contract to review. He looked me up and down with a smirk and handed the contract back to me and said, "I'll never do business with the likes of you." And he walked away. He refused to do business with me because I am a black woman.

I was completely stunned. I stood there for half a second and then the contract slipped out of my hand and onto the receptionist's desk as I bolted to my car. I couldn't get out of there fast enough. I got into my car, shut the door, clutched the steering wheel, and just sat there as the tears poured out. I looked up to heaven and shouted, "I thought you wanted me to do this! Why won't you help me?" Moments later my cell phone rang. It was the receptionist of the facility I was sitting outside of. She said, "Come get your contract; he signed it." I nearly had heart failure! I have no idea what happened, or what made him change his

mind, but I was grateful. After that incident, though, I never made another in-person appointment, nor have I ever disclosed who owns the
company on my website. I wasn't going to be judged or marginalized
because I am black or because I am a woman.

From the beginning, I wanted my company to have the reputation
of always providing the best nurses. So, in those early years, I sent my
own friends and coworkers to go do the work I had contracted. I didn't
really have any other staff, and I knew they were the best. They didn't
mind the extra money, and I was glad to have their support.

My business grew exponentially, and very quickly I was able to
quit working the night shift. Soon I was making more money than I
knew what to do with. I really couldn't believe how it all just took off,
but it did. We've had steady growth all along the way. We've had ups
and downs, high times and low times. I've had times of struggle and
frustration. That's all part of building a business and growing. Now
I'm living a life beyond my wildest dreams. Not only can I support my
family—I'm in a position of influence and I have resources to accomplish the dreams I have for my future.

{ Q & A }

Wow. What an amazing journey! Looking back, is there anything you would have done differently along the way?

All things considered, I would have gotten my MBA the first time around, to be more proficient in business. But honestly, I didn't realize business was in my future back then. As a black woman raised in the '60s, my parents didn't teach me about how to save money or build wealth. It wasn't even painted as an option. We were encouraged to get an education and then work hard at a job. We were never told to own our own company or save or invest wisely. We didn't know black people who were running businesses. I mean, they were there; we just didn't know them. So when I started making substantial money, I spent it like crazy. In fact, I made my first million and blew it. My business was still thriving; I was just not being a good steward of my personal finances. While it was fun to have extra money and to splurge in ways I couldn't before, I had to take an honest look at myself and make some hard decisions. I was able to implement some different strategies and started focusing on ways to invest and diversify so I could sustain the new wealth I was building.

You had so much stacked against you, and you weren't raised to pursue business. How did you break limiting beliefs about yourself and your abilities?

Change starts in the mind first. So when I started attending those inspirational conferences and started changing my mind-set, that's when my life started changing. There are all kinds of voices in the world, so you have to decide which voice you are going to listen to. Faith is a huge part of my journey and seeing myself through God's eyes made me see how capable and valuable I really am. On top of that, I was just fed up with feeling stuck and limited, and also seeing my kids being limited. I tell people all the time, when you get fed up, things start changing. When you get fed up, that's when you become dangerous!

Now my kids are grown, and they are pursuing higher education, business, and setting up nonprofits. I'm so proud of them, and I believe they will do even greater things than I did!

A lot of times, when people step out in new areas, they become self-reflective and have to let go of some things from the past—even people from the past. Did you go through this, as well?

Absolutely. My family didn't have a lot of faith in me when I was younger. I never felt much support from them. And then in my forties I learned that the father I grew up with wasn't my biological father. So that was a lot. But I felt in my heart that I had received so much grace in my own life that I needed to extend grace to my family. I just decided to forgive everything from the past. See, forgiveness wipes the slate clean. It's not forgiveness if you are holding a grudge or trying to get revenge. Forgiveness doesn't necessarily mean that you have to go back to an unhealthy relationship, but in my case, the right thing was a clean slate. I love my family today more than I ever have, and my sister even works for me now. She's amazingly talented and we have a great relationship.

What advice would you give to that person who may be in the same circumstance you were in when you were working the night shift as a single mom—ready for a change but not sure what to do?

I would say, if you aren't happy and fulfilled where you are, you need to find your purpose. That's not to say there won't be hard days even when you are fulfilling your purpose. The difference is that when you are fulfilling your purpose, you have a deep passion and drive that energizes you and carries you through the difficult times.

Also, I'm a person of faith. I wouldn't be where I am without God's divine intervention, so I would say, pray and follow your heart. I would have never been as successful as I am without taking a leap of faith to step out of my comfort zone, to see and to embrace the blessing I knew was out there for me. I believe the blessed life is out there for anyone who is willing to go after it!

PATTY's POINTS

● **Focus on your goal, not your limitations.**

What I love about Lisa is her sheer drive to keep moving past every limitation. She is the type of person to look for opportunities, to think outside the box, and to never give up. Even though Lisa had a lot of negative things in her life, she remained a positive person. She didn't let it stop her that she flunked out of college the first time. She didn't let it stop her that she had a learning disability. She didn't let it stop her that she made some financial mistakes. She made it work whether it was school or child care or finding contract nurses. Even if it took her longer to reach a goal, or if it meant she had to work harder than the average person to get there, that's exactly what she would do. Lisa focused on her goal instead of her limitation. She focused her life in a positive direction, and that's the direction she went.

● **It's not what others think about you, it's what you think about you that matters most.**

Did you notice how Lisa's life began to change when she changed her thoughts about herself? We all create limits in our minds. It's so important to make time to take inventory of your thoughts so you can get rid of what isn't serving you. There's an old saying, "Whether you think you can or think you can't, you're right!" Your belief about yourself and your ability lays tracks for the direction of your life. Not only that, the way you see yourself is reflected in the way you present yourself, which affects the way others see and receive you. In the entertainment industry, if someone lacks confidence it's the first thing you see when they walk on a stage. If you aren't confident in your own abilities, why should anyone else be?

REFLECTION QUESTIONS

1. Where do you see yourself in this story? What part of Lisa's personality, character traits, or journey can you relate to or identify with?

   _____

   _____

   _____

2. What is your greatest takeaway from this story?

   _____

   _____

   _____

3. Lisa talked about being marginalized and misjudged because of her looks. Is there a time in your life where something similar happened to you? Did you allow that incident to identify you? Did you shrink back or press forward?

   _____

   _____

   _____

4. Lisa talked about the importance of changing your own thoughts about yourself. What do you think about yourself? What thoughts do you need to change?

_____

_____

_____

5

It Ain't Over 'til the Lineman Sings

The Second Act Story of Ta'u Pupu'a

He was raised humbly with eight older siblings, and as a six-foot five-inch teenager, Ta'u Pupu'a knew that the only way for him to attend college was through his football talent. Ta'u worked hard and received a full college scholarship and was subsequently drafted to the NFL. He was living the life of his dreams when an unfortunate injury became the catalyst for a surprising career change.

Here is Ta'u's second act story.

His sound, his presence, and his size
impressed me immediately. He had an amazing
childlike quality, wide-eyed and willing.
It was infectious. He was fantastic!

*—Francesca Zambello, internationally
recognized director of opera and theater*

I was five years old when my family immigrated to the US from the beautiful but small Polynesian island of Tonga. My parents wanted to create a better life for us, and America was the land of opportunity. I was the youngest of nine children, and my dad sent us ahead to the mainland with my mom while he was working temporarily in Hawaii. My mom's family had already moved to Utah, so that's where we were headed and planned to stay with them for a little while.

My grandparents owned a modest two-bedroom home with a basement, and when we arrived, we discovered that my aunt and uncle and their six kids were already staying there. Needless to say, fifteen kids in a two-bedroom house was a little crowded, but my family was close, and it was our only option at first. After a few months, we moved in with my mom's younger sister and stayed there almost a year until my father arrived and we could afford our own home.

We had a humble upbringing. I wouldn't say that we were poor because the things that were really important, we had. We were blessed with a roof over our heads and a home full of love, laughter, and singing. My grandfather loved music, and when the family would get together, he would play Tonga folk songs on the guitar. My aunts and uncles would then pull out their ukuleles and join him. Before long, the whole house would start singing and harmonizing. I would give a million dollars today to go back and experience those moments with my family just one more time.

Love for music permeated my whole family. My older brother had an interest in opera, and he would bring home records that he purchased with money he earned working. Little did I know that my brother's music tastes would have such a heavy influence on me down the road. I wasn't into opera at all at the time. I was focused on football and had been playing since I was just ten years old. It all started when a neighbor noticed how I was much bigger and taller than other kids my age. He could see I had athletic talent, and so he taught me the sport and I played it with passion.

As I got into high school and started considering college, I knew

I would need a scholarship and that football was my best and only option. I received a full scholarship to attend Weber State University. After a couple of years, I heard there were NFL tryouts at the University of Utah, so I drove with my coach and a few teammates to attend. There were several NFL coaches there that day, but Bill Belichick took a particular interest in me. He came over and talked to me several times. I went home that day with the satisfaction of knowing that I did my best, but I didn't think too much about it. Several days later, I got a call: I was invited by Coach Belichick to join the Cleveland Browns, which later became the Baltimore Ravens.

I was living the life of my dreams and, most important to me, I was able to give back to my family and help my parents financially with anything from a car for my dad to simple things like cable television so they could watch me play.

I loved football and had no desire to change my profession, but one year, right before season opening, all of that changed. We were in the middle of an intense practice when a teammate, who was about six feet eight inches and 370 pounds, came at me in full force and landed right on my foot, crushing my arch. The pain was excruciating. I knew immediately something was very wrong.

After receiving treatment and some physical therapy, I was hopeful I would recover. I planned to get back playing as soon as I could. I wanted to continue to travel with my team and do rehab on the road, but my agent could see the writing on the wall. He encouraged me to go back home for rehab. The road to recovery would be a long one. I knew he was right.

The drive from Baltimore back home to Utah was the longest drive of my life. I had a lot of time to think. I started considering how much I loved music, but I wasn't quite ready to give up football yet.

I took a full year back home to let my foot recover and finally the time came when I was healed enough to play again. I spoke with Coach Belichick, who suggested that I go play for Canada first and they would pick me up from there. So that's what I did. However, in Canada I got injured again. I was so disappointed and frustrated after investing so much time and effort into my football career. One rainy afternoon sitting in a hotel room, I looked up to heaven and said, "What am I supposed to do?" Immediately the thought came to my mind: *Move forward. Move to New York and go sing.*

I was never one to second-guess myself and I didn't have any other options, so that's what I decided to do. It just felt like the right next step. When I told my friends and family, most of them were very excited. However, my grandmother, my mother, and my father were all very afraid. They had never been to New York. They only knew what they saw on TV, which portrayed the city as very dangerous and difficult. My mother cried and cried when I told her what I was going to do.

The day came for me to go and as I said good-bye, my grandmother stopped me at the door: "Wait just a minute." She went to her room and came back and placed a hundred-dollar bill in my hand. She said, "Take this." I refused, knowing she needed it more than I did, but she insisted. "We don't know what New York will be like, so take this in case you need it." I didn't want to take her money. I knew it was her emergency money, but I could tell it would give her peace of mind to know she did something for me. And since she would not take no for an answer, I received it graciously. Later on, I tried to give it back to her, but she would never take it. I still have that same hundred-dollar bill today and it's a wonderful reminder of the love and support I received from my family.

With only one suitcase and my car, I moved to New York ready to start the next chapter of my life. When I arrived, I really had no idea what to do. I found a place to stay and tried to formulate some sort of a plan. But how does one become an opera singer, exactly? I relied on what I learned from my years of playing football. First, you have to get around people who know the ropes and who are successful at what it is that you want to do, and you study them. Then you have to make connections with the right people in the industry. So I walked around Lincoln Center, which is the world's leading performing arts center, home to the Metropolitan Opera House and the Juilliard School. This is where you would find the world's top opera performers. I thought about what type of job I could get in the area that would get me around musicians and singers. Everywhere I looked there were restaurants, so I applied at a restaurant right across the street. Not only did I have a chance to meet the right professionals, I knew that every time I walked out the doors, I would see Juilliard and the Opera House and be reminded of my dream for the future.

I got a job as a seating host so that I could greet and interact with every person who walked in the door. Sure enough, renowned conductors, directors, performers, and singers would come in nightly. I would observe and study them the way I was taught to study other players in my football days. When students from Juilliard would come in, I asked a lot of questions. "Who is your teacher? Where do you sing?" I watched great performers, like Placido Domingo, and noticed what he would order and what he would eat, because diet affects your vocal cords. I noticed the singers would always lean in to speak to someone so they would not have to talk loudly or strain their voices. They would not drink alcohol at all because it would dry out their voices.

At the same time I was working at the restaurant, I started looking for a vocal coach. I had a friend who told me about a smaller opera company that would give me a chance to perform, even though it was a nonpaying role. I auditioned for them and received the part of lead tenor, and that solidified everything for me. I loved it so much, there was no way I could do anything else. I never looked back from that first opera, even though I still had a long way to go before I could make a career out of it.

Three years later, I was still working at the restaurant and trying to learn and get connected, but it wasn't easy at all. Then in 2008, everything changed for me again. I found out that the world-renowned soprano Dame Kiri Te Kanawa would be signing books in the Met Opera Shop. She is from New Zealand and, coincidentally, she is also Polynesian. The day of the book signing, I stood in line for an hour waiting for my turn to meet her. As I got closer to the front of the line, she looked up at me and noticed that I was Polynesian and asked, "Do you live here?"

I replied, "Yes."

She said, "What do you do?"

I stood tall and proud as a peacock, and with my shoulders back I announced, "I am a tenor."

She asked, "Where do you sing?"

My ego took a small hit as I replied, "Nowhere, right now."

With a compassionate, almost motherly tone she said, "It's hard here, isn't it? Is anyone helping you? I'd like to help you."

That moment was as fateful for me as the blow to my foot was years earlier, but this time it was a moment that would launch me forward, although I didn't realize it at the time. She had one of her bodyguards give me her phone number, and she told me to call her. We talked the next day. She was headed out of the country, but she said she would be back in about six months and she wanted to hear me sing.

Sure enough, about six months later she was back in town and told me to meet her at the Juilliard School to sing for her. When I arrived, she was there with Brian Zeger, the artistic director for the department of vocal arts—no pressure. I sang my heart out that day for both of them, and she was pleased by my performance. Brian commented, "We have a diamond here that needs some polishing."

She looked at Brian and said, "Brian, what can we do for this guy?"

He said, "Well, we can invite him to audition for a Juilliard scholarship to the opera center." It was a once-in-a-lifetime opportunity and well beyond anything I could have made happen on my own.

I spent the next month preparing for the audition. Over a hundred applicants showed up the day of the auditions. I kept thinking, *It's game day*. I had to bring everything I had to the field, so to speak. When my name was called, I walked into a room of at least twenty stoic faculty members and a piano. I sang five operatic arias and a monologue the best I could in French, German, and Italian, and then I was dismissed. The next day, fifty of us were called back. I made the first cut! And the day after that, only thirty were called back. And then ten, and then three. The process was a lot like football tryouts. At the end of the application process, I was one of the three who received a full scholarship to Juilliard.

It was an intense season of learning and training my voice,

training my ear, learning harmonies, and learning multiple languages. I was much older than the other students and felt like I was really behind. I didn't really know how to read music very well. I didn't really know French, Italian, or Russian as well as a professional opera singer should, so I had to learn a lot very quickly. Most of the other students had been studying music all their lives, not football tackling, so I just felt very behind much of the time.

Three years later, I was the first Polynesian ever to graduate from Juilliard. Thirty of my family members came across the country to attend the graduation ceremony. You could not miss my family in the crowd because they all showed up with the most beautiful Hawaiian leis! They had at least a hundred of them, which I ended up giving out to my colleagues.

Sadly, my mother had passed away one year prior to my graduation, so she never got to see me perform professionally. I will always hold her love in my heart and I am eternally grateful for the patience, faith, and character she instilled in me.

After graduation, I made my professional debut with the San Francisco Opera. I've performed all over the world with the greatest talents of our time. For me, the most satisfaction I have is when I walk off the stage and know that I have given my all. I am eternally grateful for every opportunity I have to sing, and I hope my story inspires others to follow their most daring and surprising dreams.

$\{$ Q & A $\}$

What would you say to someone who is in the middle of a career change or transition like what you went through?

Before you really step out and take a chance on the unknown, you have to know yourself and know the passion that's within you. Your passion is what carries you when it's hard—especially when others don't believe in what you are doing. So you have to know yourself and love yourself. Your life is your journey. It's not anyone else's journey. If someone has fear, let it be their fear, not your fear. Believe in yourself.

At the same time, if you are pursuing the performing arts, or even professional sports, I would also say to consider what your coaches and teachers and other professionals in the industry are saying to you. Here in New York it's so competitive, so you have to be realistic about your expectations, and know how much risk you are willing to take for how long and at what expense.

Did you ever feel like giving up?

One thing I learned from my parents is that there is always opportunity and you have to go after it. They set the example by coming to America, and so I live by the motto "Never give up." Sure, there were difficult times and uncertain times. There were unexpected things that happened along the way. But I believe everything happens for a reason. I am a person of faith, so that is what I would hold on to when I wasn't really sure what to do next.

Have you been back to Tonga? How have your Polynesian roots impacted you as a singer?

I have been back and in fact I was recently invited to perform for the king of Tonga, but I was already scheduled to be performing in Greece. I was so disappointed to turn down that opportunity. But my Polynesian roots are very much a part of who I am today. When I sing and perform, when it's time to get dramatic, there's something I pull from the depths of the Pacific Ocean—a warm sound. A creamy sound. An intimate sound. My heritage is a part of me, so naturally it's a part of what I bring when I sing.

Is there anything you would go back and change or do differently if you had the opportunity to do so?

Not at all. You shouldn't look back with regrets, but you can learn a lot from your own history. Everything happens for its purpose. My past experience has strengthened me for each next chapter, not only professionally, but for life in general.

PATTY's POINTS

● **Look at what you have, not at what you don't have.**

Ta'u is one of these people who just knows how to make the most out of what he has. Perhaps it was because he had so little growing up that he wasn't distracted or overwhelmed by too many options like a lot of people tend to be today. As a young man considering college, when he assessed his life and future, instead of getting frustrated about the lack of options due to his family's limited financial resources, he looked at what he could do and what he had to work with, which was his football talent. He poured himself into football and became the best he could be simply because he didn't see any other option. Ultimately, the economic challenges his family faced in sending Ta'u to college ended up giving him the resolve that directed him to his first act, a career in the NFL. His journey is a reminder that often what we see as a setback can actually be what prepares us for our future, if we only keep our perspective in the right place and focus on what we have to work with.

● **No experience is ever wasted.**

Even though Ta'u's football dream came to a sudden halt, his NFL career developed traits that he would later use to become an opera singer, traits that will serve him the rest of his life. As unconventional as it seems, his methodical approach to becoming a singer was forged while playing football.

Too often we can see an experience as a "waste of time" if it didn't get us to where we thought we were supposed to go. But if we choose to be fully present in the moment and train ourselves to look at every circumstance as a learning experience, then we never need to waste precious energy on regret. Each day can be one of discovery and growth.

● Feed your dreams.

When Ta'u moved to New York, he went straight to Lincoln Center. He chose a place to work, not for prestige or money, but where he could see the opera house every day, connect with people in the industry, and feed his dream. Think about that for a moment. He went from the pinnacle of a football career to a starter job as a host at a restaurant. That takes tremendous humility to climb the ladder of success and then go back to an entry-level position. I would imagine outsiders looked at it as a massive step back in his career. But Ta'u wasn't looking at where he was in that moment, he was making decisions based on what he needed in order to get to where he wanted to be. He knew his job was just a baby step along the way, and so it didn't matter how much money he was making or how prestigious it was. The intangible value of being able to study and learn from people in the industry far outweighed anything else.

It's so important to surround yourself with things, and people, who will feed your dreams and remind you of where you are headed—even if it means doing things that seem unconventional like taking a job below your skill set. Our lives will move in the direction of our focus. Ta'u knew this.

● Practice gratitude.

Sometimes we see that a difficult childhood is the spark that ignites a life change, but in Ta'u's case, it was the values he learned from his happy childhood that enabled him to pursue his second act. He learned to sacrifice and take risks, and although his family was not rich in material wealth, Ta'u's upbringing was rich in love. His family was grateful for each other and what they had and took great pleasure in doing simple things together, like making music.

Maybe you didn't come from a family that instilled these values in you. It's never too late to develop them on your own. Even scientists say that gratitude is important. Research demonstrates that gratitude is associated with:

- Greater happiness
- More positive emotions
- New and lasting relationships
- Better health
- More progress toward personal goals
- Fewer physical aches and pains
- More alertness and determination
- Increased generosity and empathy
- Better sleep
- Improved self-esteem

With no downside to practicing more gratitude, it seems like a goal we should all embrace.

REFLECTION QUESTIONS

1. Where do you see yourself in this story? What part of Ta'u's personality, character traits, or journey can you relate to or identify with?

   _____

   _____

   _____

2. What is your greatest takeaway from this story? List a lesson learned.

   _____

   _____

   _____

3. Like Ta'u made sure to keep the opera house before his eyes in order to feed his dream, what is something that inspires you that you can set before your eyes as a reminder of your dream or goal?

   _____

   _____

   _____

4.	Is gratefulness a part of your lifestyle? List five things you are grateful for. Perhaps start a gratefulness journal and make daily entries to help keep your perspective in the right place.

_____

_____

_____

_____

_____

6

Serving Up What Life Dished Out

The Second Act Story of Larry and Sara Bruce

Larry Bruce ran a successful landscaping business while his wife, Sara, led an interior design business. They lived in a very small town in East Texas. When the housing market crashed in 2008 and people started looking for ways to save money on services like what Larry and Sara offered were the first to go. The financial crisis hit their businesses hard and Larry and Sara found themselves looking for additional work. More than that, they knew they needed some sort of a survival plan if things got worse. They decided to cultivate their eight acres of family property and grow food, knowing that, no matter what, they could eat, and they could perhaps build a business off the bounty.

Today, they have a thriving hospitality business including a charming farm-to-table restaurant, boutique-style rental cabins, and a local meal delivery service. Larry Bruce Gardens and Farm-to-Table Restaurant has been growing since it opened and has been featured in local media as a Texas hot spot!

Here is Larry and Sara's second act story.

I grew up in the tiny Texas town of Kennard, population 319. Yes, there were probably more people in the last movie theater you went to. Sara and I met nearly forty-seven years ago, when her family bought property in the area. We actually met in the very living room of the house where we currently live. The house used to belong to my grandparents, and one day I went to visit them and saw my cousin in the living room with his cute girlfriend, Sara. She was obviously taken and a bit young for me, but seven years later, she wasn't! She became mine and we were married in 1979.

Like any typical young couple might do, Sara and I immediately moved out of our hometown to Houston, the nearest metropolitan city, seeking opportunity and a place to start a family. It wasn't as easy as we thought it would be. We were a bit naïve and a little too trusting. I took a job handling life insurance sales for another man's accounting and bookkeeping firm, but ironically, he couldn't keep up with his own payroll. In fact, he was pretty crooked and owed me about $5,000 in back salary. When I finally realized that he was never actually going to pay me, I decided to quit. Sara had just given birth to our first child, April, and we found ourselves flat broke and without a lot of options. In 1983, we were done with the big city, so we packed all of our worldly possessions into a borrowed horse trailer and decided to move to Crockett, Texas, which was closer to home but still far enough away to maintain our independence. I tried to find work to recover from the huge financial loss we had just experienced, but I couldn't catch up on the bills and our car was repossessed.

I was determined to find a way to get us back up on our feet. I saw an ad that the local grocery store was hiring. I didn't care if I had to bag groceries, I was going to do something to try to provide for our family. The store was within walking distance, so I applied for a job and they hired me as store manager. I learned all the ins and outs of produce and food ordering and handling. I made enough money to get by and eventually saved up to purchase two bicycles so we could get around town. In the winter months, Sara would sometimes pick ice out of my mustache before kissing me hello after I rode home at night because it was so cold. It certainly wasn't ideal, but it's what we had to do in order to make it. Eventually, our daughter April was old enough to sit in a child's seat on the back of the bike. This meant that Sara could pedal her to day care and start working again herself.

One day, a neighbor offered to give me a broken lawn mower. He said, "If you can fix it, you can have it." I wasn't one to look a gift horse in the mouth, even if it was a little run-down. It cost me twenty dollars to fix, and I started mowing lawns to earn extra money in my off time. By that time, we had purchased a used car and I would haul the mower in the trunk to my yard jobs.

I could see the potential in running my own lawn care business. Sara could, too, so she started working with me. I quit my job at the grocery store and started doing lawn care and landscaping full-time. With Sara's eye for design, we built a solid business together.

In 1992, well after my grandparents passed away, we were offered the opportunity to buy their property. We couldn't afford to buy all of the land, so we bought the house and one acre. It was special to us. Not only was it my grandparents' land and the place where we met, the land had been in the family since the 1800s. My great-great-grandfather raised his family here, my great-grandfather raised his family here, my grandfather raised his family here, and now I would raise my family here, too. Over the subsequent years, we were able to eventually purchase the remaining seven acres.

I ran our landscaping business off that property while Sara built her interior design business. We were doing well, but when 2008 came along, everything changed. Thankfully, we were out of debt for several years before the recession hit. Otherwise, we would have personally had a complete crash. Both of our businesses started spiraling as people tightened their purse strings to make it through. As we watched our bank account go down, we thought about what we could do to earn a living and survive. There was a lot of fear. There was even talk about a global collapse on the news. We knew that no matter what, everybody has to eat. So we started a garden behind the house. We were sitting on pins and needles waiting for the first crops to come in. We still had occasional work with our other businesses, but it wasn't going to last, and taking care of the garden started taking more of our time.

Our first produce was a beautiful crop of lettuce. Sara was so excited! She tried to sell it to the local grocery store, but they weren't interested. We couldn't believe they didn't want fresh, local produce. Then she went to the schools to see if she could sell them fresh produce for school lunches, and they weren't interested either. She tried everywhere she could think of and ran into rejection after rejection. I had an idea. I said, "Sara, do you think you could make a salad with that lettuce and sell it as a meal?" She agreed to try it. She immediately made a taco salad and posted a photo of it on Facebook, which was brand-new at the time. Sure enough, people commented on the photo about how good it looked and that they wanted to buy it. So we started delivering prepared meals locally. That taco salad was our first income off the land.

Other crops were coming in and we had a lot of excess produce, so I went to Texas A&M University and got certified in canning and preserving. I thought this would be something I could teach people so they could preserve their own food and be prepared in the event of an emergency.

In 2010, we enclosed the concrete slab of our basketball court and built a commercial kitchen with two huge, family-style high-top tables. We could seat about twenty-eight people, and we envisioned doing canning classes and cooking and preparing our own fruits and vegetables and meals for delivery in that space. Then I got on the local radio station and started advertising what we were doing. Our delivery business grew, but we discovered there really wasn't a market for canning classes. We weren't chefs, but Sara had an idea. Not far from us, in Houston, is a branch of the number one culinary institute in the country. What if we could get someone from the school to come cook meals on-site? So that was our next step. We brought in instructors from the school and started hosting farm-to-table dinners on the weekends in our commercial kitchen. The meals were fabulous—and the produce was fresh. Word started spreading quickly. We outgrew seating in our commercial kitchen and had to plan for a way to expand.

In 2013, we built on a more formal dining room, and the people kept coming. For holidays and events, we were beyond maxed out, so we tried outdoor seating around the garden. The weather rarely cooperated and the mosquitoes in Texas are big enough to carry you off, so we knew we had to make plans to expand our indoor dining again to accommodate the growth. We couldn't believe how people were just finding us. They were coming from everywhere. Mostly by word of mouth. Over the next few years, we added on three more dining rooms. By this time, we hired on a team of chefs and service personnel, and we were back using our skill sets in design and construction to expand and run the restaurant.

In 2015, we inherited some one-bedroom cottages that a family member previously used as rental properties. Well, really they were shacks! But we moved four of them to our property, remodeled and redecorated them, and listed them on Airbnb. Sara and I really didn't know what to expect, but our daughter April is a realtor and really encouraged us in this direction. We couldn't imagine why anyone would want to come out to the middle of nowhere and pay to spend the night here, but to our surprise, the units started renting out immediately. Turns out, people love to escape to the country. We now have eight "guest houses" that are regularly occupied.

Today, we deliver more than one hundred meals daily and serve more than three hundred farm-to-table dinners on-site every weekend. We are set up buffet style with live entertainment, banjos, and bluegrass. We are completely maxed out again and have to turn people away on holidays. Now with the rental cottages, we are a full hospitality business and enjoy it immensely! We never imagined our lives would go in this direction, but we couldn't be happier. We've also attracted the attention of local media. We were featured in *Texas Highways* magazine, *Texas Monthly*, *Texas Farm and Home*, *Texas Country Reporter*, the *Texas Bucket List*, and by local radio and TV stations.

We've definitely had our challenges, but moving forward one step at a time, solving problems one at a time, and a heaping dose of grace has carried us to where we are today.

{ Q & A }

What advice would you give to someone looking to make a change in life?

Larry: First and foremost, you have to be flexible. Whether you have a plan or not, you have to know that things may or may not turn out the way you expect.

We didn't have a plan. We found ourselves in the middle of a global financial crisis. We never considered a restaurant until it was one step ahead of us. We were just trying to figure out how to make money with what we had in our hands.

You have to look for opportunities when you are trying to reinvent yourself. You may be told "no" over and over, but you can't let that stop you. Look for the "yes" in life.

What would you say was the most difficult obstacle to overcome?

Larry: Well, you have to remember that our immediate town is only three hundred people. Most of our clientele are from neighboring towns. When we made the first expansion out of the kitchen, we required reservations so we could know exactly how many people to expect and how much food to prepare. We didn't have a menu to order from because everyone received the same thing. Around here, people didn't go to restaurants that were reservation only. We quickly developed a reputation for being too "high-falutin'" for the area. To make matters worse, one day, while we were doing the second expansion, Sara had to quickly buy light fixtures because she didn't realize the electrician was coming the next day. Around here, you don't reschedule, or they may never come back. She jumped online to an auction website and found six crystal chandeliers for ten dollars apiece. She couldn't tell how big they were from the photo but bought them because they were so inexpensive. So I drove down to Houston in my Expedition to pick them up and when I got there, I couldn't even fit one in my car, let alone six! They were enormous! I had to go back with a dump truck to get them all. Well, when people saw these new massive chandeliers, they thought we were really overdoing it, like a Vegas hotel or something. So, our most difficult obstacle? We had to overcome reservations and chandeliers . . . aka: the mentality of a small town.

At one point, our neighbors went into meltdown mode because they didn't like all the traffic. We had a parking lot on-site, so no one was parking in the streets or blocking any driveways or access roads. But someone complained to the local TV station, and the local TV station called the fire department. The caller told them we washed our produce in sewage water, which is completely untrue. So the fire department called the EPA and then the local police. Eventually we got it all straightened out.

How did you stay encouraged during so much uncertainty?
Larry: First and foremost, we found rest in our faith. But we also told each other: failure is not an option. For this to work, we had to work. We made it our business to know how to do everything on this property. We both did it all. We now have ten or twelve staff members working with us, but our confidence in what we were doing came because we know every single job on our property, and we made sure it all got done right.

Did you have any marked moments where you just knew you were on the right path?
Sara: That's a good question, and yes, many. But one particular story comes to mind.

It was New Year's Day 2014, and we planned to do nothing and have a lazy day, since they are few and far between. Well, the phone rang and it was a guy at the gate that we'd never met before who wanted to meet us and see our restaurant. We agreed to meet him out in the kitchen and he stayed about thirty minutes. Then he asked if he could pray for us. We weren't sure yet if he was some sort of nut, but we were polite and prayed with him . . . with one eye open. And then he said, "I have a grand piano I'd like to let you borrow. I need a place for it to stay and if you'd like to use it, I'll pay to have it moved here and tuned up."

We were absolutely floored. Larry plays the piano, so we immediately said, "Yes!"

What's something you gave up that you never thought you would?

Larry: Travel. We don't go anywhere right now. It's been a complete change in lifestyle. It's not a burden at this time because we genuinely love what we do. But at some point that's going to have to change. For now, we call this our own personal resort. Sara is also responsible for her mother's welfare, so her downtime is really limited.

Did you go through a period of "midlife crisis"? What did that look like and how did you resolve it?

Larry: Well this is so much better than anything we could have thought of. Back in 2001, our landscaping was booming. I had so much work, I couldn't get anywhere fast enough. I felt like I was going to have a nervous breakdown about once a year. I actually told Sara, "One day I would love it if all I had to do was walk out the back door and I'd be at work." Now I'm living that out. So for me, this change saved me from a midlife crisis!

Sara: I don't think I would call it a "crisis," but I had a lot of panic moments along the way. For example, when we first started delivery, one day we were working our butts off, and I got up to check the bank account balance and it was twenty-eight cents! I hustled to sell some lunches that day to keep us from going in the red. Our overhead was always big because we didn't know what we were doing. We tried so hard to be a success, and so many times it was discouraging; but we weren't ever going to throw in the towel.

What would you tell your younger self now?

Larry: I would say, "Seek wisdom." I kept trying to figure it out all on my own as if we were reinventing the wheel. If I could go back, I would pay more attention to the little things. Sara has a second cousin who is a very famous cowboy. The first time I met him I heard him say, "The secret to success is to pay attention." It's those little details where you are losing money.

Sara: I would tell myself to be calm and peaceful. Trust God. His ways are always going to be better.

PATTY's POINTS

● **Develop a "whatever it takes" attitude.**

What leaps out at me about Larry and Sara's story is their willingness to do whatever necessary to make ends meet. How many people today would be willing to ride a bike in the winter to get to a job they didn't really want to do? I don't think I would! But that is the kind of character and determination that brought Larry and Sara to where they are today. It's quite admirable and inspiring.

Larry and Sara were willing to sacrifice to achieve their goals. Besides working hard, they've also had to go without: as Larry mentions, travel is one thing they have not been able to do. Fortunately, they love their business, so it's not a truly painful sacrifice. But Larry also states that at some point that will need to change. However, like so many people in this book, loving what they are doing in their second act makes these sacrifices bearable.

● **Be willing to adapt to what life hands you.**

All through their journey, Larry and Sara had to learn to constantly adapt, whether it meant adapting to the downturn in the national economy or to their neighbor's complaints. They had to completely change gears when the financial crisis of 2008 hit. Their lawn care business collapsed, so they used what they had—their own backyard—to move into growing vegetables. Even so, they had to try a number of times before figuring out a way to make money from their garden.

Notice also that when vendors kept telling them "no" to their produce, they didn't keep knocking on doors that were closed. Instead, they kept looking for the "yes." They kept exploring other ideas and didn't stop until they found something that worked. How many people would have thrown in the towel when the local grocer turned them down? Their flexibility fueled their success.

Teamwork makes the dream work.

I also love how Larry and Sara displayed a real sense of teamwork, which is so important to keep up spirits when the going gets tough. The story of Sara kissing Larry's frozen mustache as he rode his bike home from work in the winter is such a lovely and telling detail about their relationship. Having a sense of being on the journey together, with all the ups and downs, lightens the burden of the setbacks. Having someone to lean on, to bounce ideas off of, to get encouragement from is so important. Even if you aren't married, don't be afraid to ask for help or seek wisdom from your family, friends, and circle of influence.

Tap into social resources.

Social media, though it can often expose the darker side of humanity, is also a source of constant blessing for people like Larry and Sara who need to reach a target audience quickly and cheaply. Posting one picture of her taco salad on Facebook launched the couple's now successful restaurant and B&B business. Facebook, Instagram, Twitter, and other platforms are a terrific way to test the waters for new ideas, create community, launch products and services, discuss ideas, and exchange information.

REFLECTION QUESTIONS

1. Where do you see yourself in this story? What part of Larry and Sara's personalities, character traits, or journey can you relate to or identify with?

   _____

   _____

   _____

2. What is your greatest takeaway from this story?

   _____

   _____

   _____

3. As a young couple, Larry and Sara set out to the big city and were taken advantage of in a way that left them destitute. They had to go back before they could go forward. Have you ever found yourself going backward in life? When you consider what happened in your life, is it holding you back in any way?

   _____

   _____

   _____

7

The Visual Effects of
an Autism Mom

The Second Act Story of Yudi Bennett

Yudi Bennett had the career of her dreams working in the film industry. As a member of the Directors Guild, she worked as an assistant director on many prominent film and television projects in Hollywood. But when her son received a diagnosis of autism spectrum disorder in 1997 her world changed. It was a time when the internet was in its infancy and there were very few resources to help.

She and her husband became trailblazers in the autism community, establishing programs and resources to educate parents. Years later, Yudi and her team did something no one else in the world was doing. Seeing the massive need for employment among the autistic population, Yudi found a way for adults with autism to work in the film industry. Today, through her organization, Exceptional Minds, talented teams of visual effects artists and animators, all of whom have autism, work on projects such as *Avengers: Endgame*, *Black Panther*, and *Game of Thrones*. She's taking the employment problem head-on and paving the way for other organizations to carry the torch on behalf of the 80 percent of adults with autism who are unemployed.

Here is Yudi's second act story.

I never planned on having a second act. I loved my first act and intended to keep working for as long as possible. I had a really great career working as an assistant director in film production for over thirty years. I gave my heart and soul to my job and was honored to be a recipient of the prestigious Frank Capra Achievement Award, which recognizes people in my field for career achievement and service to the Directors Guild of America.

I remember my father telling me how fortunate I was to have landed in a career field that I loved so much because most people start in the workforce and move around a few times before they settle into their long-term career. That wasn't me. I thought they'd have to have my funeral on a set because I wasn't planning to ever leave my job. However, life had other plans for me. Some people find a second act, but in my case, my second act found me.

In 1997, our son Noah was diagnosed with autism. He was three years old at the time. It all seemed to happen so suddenly. At two years old he was talking and saying "Mama" and "Dada," but at three years old he stopped. He reverted back to just making sounds. This was more than two decades ago and nobody really knew anything about autism. When you said the word, people would shudder. There was very little internet and few books to read. It was a very terrifying time.

My husband and I, with all of our education, resources, and resourcefulness, were struggling, so we couldn't imagine how other parents were coping—and even more so if English wasn't your native tongue. There was a lot of bureaucracy you had to navigate in order to get services for your child. My husband, Bob Schneider, decided to start an autism support organization for parents called Foothill Autism Alliance, which is still operating today. We incorporated as a nonprofit and held monthly meetings because we knew there were a lot of desperate parents out there just getting the diagnosis. The rate kept climbing over the years—from 1 in 10,000 to suddenly 1 in 150 and today it's 1 in 53. Kids were being diagnosed right and left, so we knew a lot of parents were looking for answers. My husband was the president and driving force of the organization, but I began to cut back on work a little bit to help him.

Five years later, Bob, the love of my life, died of cancer.

At that point, I had a huge decision to make. How could I take care of my son and work twelve- to fourteen-hour days in the film industry? I never imagined a life without Bob. It marked a turning point in my life.

It took some time to process everything, but after I pulled myself together, I took over his role as president of the alliance. During the time he was fighting cancer, he put together a four-hundred-page resource guide, which I updated. We distributed 3,500 free copies to families all over Los Angeles to show them what to do and where to get services. It became the "Autism Bible" for Los Angeles. Around that time, I slowly left the film industry and started caring for my child full-time.

Right after our son was diagnosed, I remember Bob looking at me and saying, "What is he going to do when he grows up?" From the very beginning, it was always in the back of our minds that we needed to think of our son's future. We didn't know anyone with autism at the time. Where were they all? What were they doing as adults? We weren't seeing them on movie sets or at the grocery store. My husband was always forward-thinking, so we would talk about ideas and what we could do for our son. We wondered if we should be setting up a business for him and, if so, what would that be? Autism is very complicated; they say if you've met one person with autism, you've met one person with autism. It manifests itself very differently in different people, so it's difficult to make generalities or draw conclusions or make long-term plans. We knew we had to do something for him, we just had no idea what. And now I was left to figure it out on my own.

A number of years went by, and Noah was struggling in middle school. One day, another parent who I met through the alliance told me about an after-school animation program for kids with autism that was taught by a very gifted teacher. She recommended we give it a try. Noah applied for the program and then had to go through an interview process. When I took him in for the interview, the instructor told me he wasn't sure that the program was a right fit. He didn't think my son could learn the Adobe software or handle the assignments. I wasn't really sure what to expect either, but we decided to give it a shot. Three weeks later, my son knew the software inside and out. It was like a lightbulb was turned on inside of him. He loved the program! He loved animation and computer graphics and his whole world started changing. He started doing noticeably better in school. His social interactions improved, and he was overall a happier kid. What was really remarkable is that his language started coming back, and he developed a love for drawing, which he never had before. It was a turning point for him and it was really eye-opening for me. All the kids in the program seemed to light up and it was something they looked forward to each week.

Along with my son and other middle and high school students, there were students in the program who had already graduated high school. They didn't have jobs or anything to do during the day, so they would sit around the house doing nothing, waiting for this after-school computer animation class to roll around once or twice each week. It was really tragic because they had no future ahead of them, and it made me sad to think of the lack of options for people like my son.

I met with the other parents, and we started talking about what it would look like to have a full-time program and actually train young adults to work professionally in the film industry. We started exploring the idea more deeply and learned there was a need for visual effects artists and animators. So that became our goal: to develop a training program for adults with autism to have meaningful careers in the visual effects and animation arena.

In 2009, we incorporated Exceptional Minds as a nonprofit, formed a board of directors, and then opened our school in September 2011. Because of my background as an assistant director, I knew how to organize and get things done, so I initially worked as a volunteer handling the administrative work that was needed to get the program up and running. We set it up as a three-year vocational program right from the beginning. We hired highly qualified teachers and industry professionals to work with the students. Everyone was excited to be a part of something so life-changing for these young adults.

It was rewarding work, even though it was challenging at times, and there were a lot of hurdles to overcome in the early years. For one thing, we had to raise enough money to make the project viable. We were fortunate to receive several grants as well as seed money from a private donor. We started with a group of nine students, but we had some attrition in the beginning because we had not yet developed a rigorous assessment process. One of our students left after the first year because he wanted to write screenplays. Another one dropped out because his parents had talked him into the program but he really wasn't interested. This was a common and heartbreaking problem . . . there are so few programs and parents are desperate. We soon learned to interview prospective students without the parents in the room and we created a hands-on computer assessment to evaluate the candidates' technical abilities and interests.

We also had to learn to navigate the dynamic technical culture because software changes so fast. We would start teaching one type of software and then learn that another software was released and in demand. So we did the best we could to adapt and learned a lot along the way.

We also knew that after three years, our students weren't going to simply walk into a studio and get a job. The film industry is one of the most competitive industries in the world. So as the first class was going into their third year, we opened our own in-house production studio that was run by a friend of mine who was a talented visual effects producer with twenty years of experience. This would mean we could bring the work in to our students, rather than sending them out to find jobs.

Setting up the studio was no easy feat. In order to accept work from the studios, we had to become vetted by the Motion Picture Association. The vetting process is quite intense and there's a lot of

security involved because nobody wants their movies leaked early to
YouTube or Facebook. Eventually we were cleared and able to bid on
jobs like any other production house. If we could bid appropriately
and competitively, we could earn the business. That's not to say some
people didn't want to use us simply because of who we were, but we
had to show that we could deliver on time and with really high-quality
work. In the film industry, the bottom line is: Can you get it done on
time and as cheaply as possible? We worked hard to convince people to
give us a shot because we knew the only way to get our students a job
outside the studio was to give them lots of experience in our in-house
studio. Once we had one production job, our goal was to get repeat
business from that studio. We would celebrate every time a company
would ask us to do a second job because that's how we really knew our
model was working.

It was pretty nerve-racking in the beginning when we first got
started and had to prove ourselves as a studio. We always worried
about deadlines for every production job because we knew we were
only as good as our last job—we had to deliver on time, every time,
no matter what it took. But our guys weren't working alone; we had
professional paid supervisors just like they would have at any other
production facility. The difference with us is that in any other facility
you might have one supervisor for fifteen artists, but we had one supervisor for about five artists.

In the early days, we did some end credit rolls for independent
features and some visual effects cleanup for 20th Century Fox on one
of the *Planet of the Apes* sequels. It was limited work, but we were so
grateful to get a foot in the door. But what really took us to the next
level was when Marvel Studios started hiring us. We worked on all of
their superhero movies, which, of course, thrilled our students.

It took a while before our first graduate was employed outside of
the studio. Marvel hired one of our guys to work for them full-time,
and it was so successful that they've come back to hire more. We have
several graduates working there full-time. Marvel has really been a
wonderful supporter of our program. Also, Stargate Studios hired a

visual effects artist from us right after he graduated from the program, which was exciting. We have an extremely robust work readiness program where we teach the social skills needed for the work environment. At first, we were teaching those skills one day a week, but we soon embedded that into the program every single day because we realized the challenge is learning the soft skills, not the technical skills. Our students learn the software really fast. The problem is all the unwritten "rules of the work world," the subtle things you need to know—like what body language means, or how to behave in an office, or how to take feedback and get along with your coworkers. Things that everybody getting out of college might struggle with to some degree, but our students really struggle with. So we spent a huge amount of time focusing on work readiness. All of this factors in when they apply for a job. Now we are partnering with studios for summer internships, which are optional, but we really encourage all of our students to take advantage of these opportunities. We just partnered with Cartoon Network on a mentorship program to help our students be more prepared for the workforce when they graduate. Because of opportunities like these, some of our students will get jobs immediately and won't have to work at our studio first. In the early days, about 90 percent of graduates needed the on-the-job experience with us.

One of my favorite things is giving tours of the facility. You can see the look of amazement on visitors' faces because our studio looks just like any other studio. Everyone is focused and working away on their shots. There's nothing anywhere that cries "autism." I've had people come to the studio and actually ask me, "Now, which ones have autism?" And I say, "All of them." It's the same way with our classrooms. They look like any other classrooms. I don't know what people are expecting, but I'm so proud of our students, graduates, and faculty. There's a thing about human nature, and it's true in the autistic community as well. When people are doing what they love, they rise to the occasion. They are motivated and focused. So kids who may have acted out in high school, because they were studying subjects they didn't like, have a complete turnaround when they start doing what they actually like.

> When people are doing what they love,
> they rise to the occasion.

We have a very elaborate interview process now because we have about three times as many applicants as we do spots in the program. We need to see that a student really wants to be here. Passion is one of the biggest admissions. An applicant's level of desire determines their level of engagement, which really determines their level of success with the program.

Every day we get requests from all over the world, not just the US, because there is such a shortage of employment programs for adults with autism. We never wanted to be the only one; we wanted to be a model for other people to start programs in other fields. It's estimated that 80 to 90 percent of adults with autism are unemployed and many of the 20 percent who are employed don't earn enough to support themselves. This is tragic in a time where, overall, employment is at an all-time low, under 4 percent in the general population. For it to be 80 percent or more in this group is alarming. But it's also complicated. It's hard to develop a one-size-fits-all program because one size really doesn't fit all most of the time.

Now I've turned over the reins of Exceptional Minds and I'm working with a couple of other nonprofits in the same arena to help expand the job market for autistic adults. One of the nonprofits I volunteer with is called the Uniquely Abled Project. UAP trains adults with autism to work in manufacturing as computer numerically controlled (CNC) operators. CNC operators are tasked with monitoring machinery, inspecting finished products, and leading test runs. The job requires a high attention to detail and excellent mechanical aptitude.

This program has been wildly successful because there's a dire need in that industry. Manufacturing doesn't get the publicity like Exceptional Minds does because it's not as "sexy" as working in Hollywood, but Uniquely Abled Project has almost a 100 percent placement rate due to the shortage of people going into manufacturing nationwide. This program is also replicable all over the country, whereas Exceptional Minds really only works in LA.

I'm also still heavily involved with the Foothill Autism Alliance, which we started twenty-two years ago. Back then, the parents in the group all had three- and four-year-olds. Now we have adult children in their twenties, so we've shifted our focus in the last few years to teens and adults. There are a lot of options nowadays for younger kids through other organizations, but this demographic, teens and adults, is largely underserved. Over the next decade, an estimated 500,000 autistic teens (50,000 each year) will enter adulthood and age out of school-based autism services. The cost of caring for Americans with autism had reached $268 billion in 2015 and is expected to rise to $461 billion by 2025 in the absence of more effective interventions and support across the life span. Autism doesn't just affect those with the diagnosis—it affects all of us.

Foothill Autism Alliance is also running workshops on employment and housing and critical issues in the autism world. Not only do these adults need skills for jobs, they also need places to live. Whereas there are already programs carved out to help veterans and the homeless, there's no affordable housing programs for people with developmental disabilities. So we're trying to get something organized to create affordable housing for this population. Right now, 80 percent of adults with autism live with their parents into their forties and fifties. But their parents will eventually get too old to take care of them, and they don't have any options. They have never even lived anywhere else. We need to teach independence and provide opportunities for them to live on their own to the best of their capabilities.

By and large, we're playing catch-up within the autism community. They have developed programs and services for school-age kids with autism, for the most part, but that's only twelve years of a person's life. Nobody's been thinking about what's going to happen over the next sixty years.

I'm just one person doing what I can to make a difference. While it wasn't what I planned, I'm grateful to be doing what I'm doing and impacting these precious lives in such a tangible way. It's an exceptional opportunity to work with these exceptional minds.

My two careers are so very different that I don't think there's any way to compare them. I loved working in the movie industry because of the creativity, energy, and adventure. I loved working in a different place every day with new challenges. It was exhilarating. The nonprofit world presents different challenges. While at times it may be less exciting, you can't measure the rewards of hearing a young adult tell you that you have changed his life forever and now he feels like he is "part of society." You can't. Or when a parent tells you that they "were drowning" and you saved their life? Each career has had its own rewards, and I am grateful to have made an impact in both.

{ Q & A }

What amazing work you are doing! Such a labor of love. You said from the time your son was young, you were thinking about where he'd work when he got older. Is he now working for Exceptional Minds?

[Laughs] *Well, the interesting story here is that one thing I've learned in all of this is: You can't live your children's dreams for them. You have to live your dream and let your children live their dreams. So, my son completed the program and after graduating he worked in the studio for a year . . . and he absolutely hated visual effects. At that point, we weren't doing animation, which he probably would've enjoyed more. But he hated visual effects because there was no creative latitude. You had to do exactly what the client wanted for each frame. If they want something removed, you have to remove it. He always wanted to make it better. He decided that he really wanted to go to college and study illustration, so that's what he's doing now and he's doing really well. The film industry is my dream, and it's worked for dozens of kids and young adults, but it's not everybody's dream. My son is finding his own path, and I'm okay with that.*

Noah is a remarkable human being, especially when you consider that he didn't speak and that he struggled with school. Nobody thought he would graduate high school. But not only did he graduate, he's now attending college. And about three years ago, he went off on his own and got his driver's license. Maybe half our kids at Exceptional Minds have driver's licenses. I'm really proud of him and all he's accomplished.

What would you say was your biggest obstacle when opening the school?

It was really a challenging undertaking because we didn't have any experience running a school, let alone a school for autistic adults. Most times when you start something, you look for a model to follow. But as much as I researched, there really wasn't a model out there. There weren't any programs for adults with autism. So there was a lot of trial and error trying to figure out who were the right candidates for the program, deciding what was the right software, and what to key in on for the social skills training. When you advertise that something is "for the film industry," you get all kinds of applicants. We had kids wanting to become screenwriters, or actors—they wanted to use our program as an open door to the industry. But this is a very specialized program, for a very specific job in the industry, and we were looking for a specific type of person who wanted to do the work and be successful at it.

To help students discover if this is a right fit for them, we've added weekend programs and summer programs, starting as young as twelve years old. We had 150 kids attend last summer. It's a great way for them to learn whether or not they really want to be in this career.

The other huge challenge is convincing prospective employers to open their hearts and minds to give these talented artists a chance to thrive. We are so grateful to all the studios who are partnering with Exceptional Minds and welcoming our graduates and hope others will follow their lead.

Now that your son is grown and you've had so much experience with kids on the spectrum, what would your advice be to that mom who just got a diagnosis for her child?

I would say: Don't put limitations on your child. Don't look at the disability—look for the abilities. Put your kid in everything. I lucked out when I found that computer animation class.

Also, don't do this alone. You have to get connected with other parents. It takes a village, and you need people in your life to help you navigate everything.

What do you see for yourself over the next decade, now that your son is grown? Do you ever see yourself going back to assistant directing?

Raising a child with a developmental disability is a lifetime commitment. Just because your child graduates high school or college or turns twenty-one does not mean that the disability disappears. There's still so much we do not understand about autism. Noah has many challenges. He currently lives at home while attending college part-time. He works with a life coach to prepare him for moving out someday (hopefully in the near future!), holding down a job, and living on his own. We celebrate every move forward. Movie production is all-consuming with long hours, out-of-town travel, and unpredictability. It requires a great deal of focus. I don't think I could do both jobs simultaneously. However, I continue to stay involved in the film industry by being active in the Directors Guild and the Academy of Motion Picture Arts and Sciences.

Because I recently retired, I see myself traveling and spending more time with my family, which I haven't been able to do through the years. Until my son got his license, I couldn't leave him because he had no way of getting around, so my life was really limited. But I will continue to support the nonprofit organizations I've started. I don't see myself necessarily starting any more organizations. I want to be the person that if you have a great idea and you want to start an organization, please call me. I want to help you do that.

PATTY's POINTS

● **Embrace change.**

People who work in the entertainment industry tend to be resourceful. The changeable nature of our business requires those who work in the field to be ready to let go and move on. Combine those attributes with a mother's instinct to protect her son and you have Yudi Bennett.

Yudi saw a need in their own life and took action. She improved her life, her son's life, and the lives of hundreds of others in the process. Her influence is still growing through the programs she is helping roll out.

But what would have happened if Yudi was not the type of person to embrace change? Moving into a second act is about more than just embracing a new season of life, it's about embracing all the unexpected details of that season—roadblocks to your ideas and plans, things that can either stop you or fuel you. Yudi had many of these along the way, from her son's diagnosis, to giving up her dream career, to losing her husband. She bravely found a path around these roadblocks.

If you are the type of person who doesn't easily embrace change, start practicing. Get out of your comfort zone. Try something new, even if it's as simple as a new restaurant. Controlled change can help equip us when change happens that is beyond our control.

● **Find trusted mentors and supporters of your dream.**

The importance of guides, mentors, and supporters cannot be overstated in getting started on a second act. In Yudi's case, though her husband tragically passed away before he was able to see Exceptional Minds come to life, she talks about how his forward thinking inspired her. So, early on, Yudi had her husband's vision to see what might be possible for their son and others like him. In the same way, when she met a gifted teacher who brought her son out of his shell through teaching him computer animation, it inspired Yudi to imagine what could be achieved if her son and others with autism had access to such a program full-time.

● **You are more equipped than you know.**

Along with mentors, Yudi's own life experience was vital to creating Exceptional Minds. Out of necessity, Yudi had to leave the industry she loved to take care of her son. But her expertise and the network of relationships she developed in the entertainment industry made her the perfect person to create a studio for kids on the spectrum. Likewise, her early work in the autism community taught her how to evaluate prospective students to create a work environment in which they could flourish.

Now, if you would have told Yudi when she was in her twenties what she would be doing for her second act, she probably would have never believed it. However, each experience in her life prepared her for it.

Be very specific.

Notice that Yudi kept to a very specific mission with her program. She didn't allow other opportunities to distract her and take her off course. Like a laser, she focused her energy on a very specific goal.

As with everyone in this book, I'm so impressed by Yudi's hard work and determination. Working with movie and television studios is very difficult. The amount of technical and legal specifics that must be met are overwhelming, and yet Yudi was able to navigate it all to create a life-changing organization such as Exceptional Minds. The determination of a mother defending her child is a powerful force indeed.

REFLECTION QUESTIONS

1. Where do you see yourself in this story? What part of Yudi's personality, character traits, or journey can you relate to or identify with?

    _____

    _____

    _____

2. What is your greatest takeaway from this story?

    _____

    _____

    _____

3. On a scale of 1 to 10, with 10 being excellent, how good are you at embracing change and adapting to circumstances that are beyond your control? What are some ways you can get out of your comfort zone and stretch yourself to grow in this area?

    _____

    _____

    _____

4. Do you have some trusted mentors? Sometimes, a mentor can be
    a public figure. They don't always have to be in your close circle,
    as long as you are learning from them. List two or three mentors
    and why you believe they are a right fit. As a mentor to organiza-
    tions who want to create jobs for special-needs adults, Yudi said
    she was open to hearing from people who needed help. Have you
    considered writing to your mentors, to ask for specific guidance or
    support?

    _____

    _____

    _____

A Doctor Listens to His Own Heart

The Second Act Story of Paul Osteen, MD

For seventeen years, Dr. Paul Osteen ran a successful medical practice in Arkansas. The death of his father, a well-respected pastor in Houston, Texas, led to enormous changes in his life. After spending a season helping his family run his father's church, he now combines his skills as a surgeon and love of giving back to provide much-needed surgeries and medical care in under-resourced countries around the world. He also launched the annual Mobilizing Medical Missions (M3) Conference that brings together health care professionals to find innovative solutions to help meet pressing global health care needs.

Here is Paul's second act story.

I absolutely love surgery. It's been my passion almost my entire life. My father was a pastor, and so our family was raised with a sense of responsibility to help people. We were always mindful of ways to meet others' needs, and I chose the route of medicine.

In 1997, after seventeen years in practice as a surgeon in Arkansas,

I felt a subtle but noticeable sense of unrest inside me. At first, I tried to reason it away . . . but it wouldn't leave me. It was the kind of unrest that makes you stop and think, *What is this? Why do I feel this way?* It didn't make sense because, at the time, I was in the best place of my life. My career was thriving, my family healthy. I had been through a difficult divorce, but by then I was married again, this time to the love of my life. There was no reason not to be completely happy. Still, I could feel my passion and drive waning as the internal restlessness grew day by day.

I talked to several trusted friends, and they deduced it was either burnout or a midlife crisis. I couldn't figure out how I could be having a midlife crisis since I was living an otherwise happy and fulfilled life. I didn't know what to do about this feeling, so I just soldiered through it.

The nagging restlessness evolved into an overwhelming sense that I was supposed to do something different with the second half of my life. I had no idea what, so I just kept doing what I knew to do until a door opened to me.

That open door finally came in the most unexpected way. In 1999, I received a phone call one day from a dear friend in Houston. My father, pastor of a sizable church in Houston, who had been struggling with his health for a while, had died unexpectedly of a heart attack and stroke.

After my dad's memorial service, I was blindsided by what seemed to be an absolutely crazy thought. I'll never forget driving home from the funeral back to Arkansas on Highway 59, passing the Cleveland exit. I suddenly had this strong feeling in my heart that I knew what my next step was supposed to be. I had this sense that I was supposed to give up my practice and go support my family by taking over my dad's church—something I would have never considered prior to that moment. My younger brother, Joel, would be stepping up as pastor, so I felt that I should be there for him and my mom, and the rest of the church family. It made absolutely no sense to my mind, but it made perfect sense to my heart and the unrest I had inside. I had to tell my wife, Jennifer, what I was thinking, and I had no idea how she would respond. I said, "Jen, I feel like I know what we are supposed to do next. I think we should move to Houston and help with the church." Without hesitation she replied, "Let's do it." The moment I made the decision, that nagging restlessness went away and my heart felt settled.

We didn't start making plans officially for several weeks. I wanted to make sure that what I was thinking wasn't an emotional decision, that we were simply caught up in the moment after my dad's death. Sure enough, the thought never left either one of us even as the weeks passed. However, our circle of friends in Arkansas weren't as excited about our plans as we were. I told my pastors, and they tried to talk me out of it. They thought it was a knee-jerk reaction to my dad's death. They weren't optimistic at all. In fact, they thought I was making a huge mistake. The other surgeons in our practice were supportive but sad. They didn't want to see me go. But what struck me the most deeply was the response from my patients who asked, "Why are you leaving your ministry here to go to a different ministry?" It was so hard because they looked up to me for more than surgery in many ways. I had counseled many families through difficult medical journeys, and they tried to convince me not to go. That inner confidence I had made all the difference. I had to rely on what I knew in my heart and not let what others thought or said deter me.

The next July, six months later, we made the move from our sleepy town in Arkansas to the fourth-largest city in the nation. It was a pretty drastic change in lifestyle and income. It was exciting and wonderful, but at the same time, I secretly second-guessed myself for about two years. I felt pretty disconnected as I tried to find the rhythm in my new world. The people I left behind in Arkansas really didn't understand why I was leaving, and the people in Houston didn't really know or understand where I was coming from. I left so much behind. My number one emotional gift is harmony, and my harmony was disrupted.

On top of that, the church grew from about five thousand to forty-five thousand over a six-year period. That was well beyond anyone's expectation. It was incredible, but it was also overwhelming. Just when I would find my bearings and get into a rhythm, everything would change as the church's growth continued. Not only that, I wasn't used to my life being in the public eye. It felt like a lot of pressure at times, and there were a couple of occasions when I wanted to quit and go back to surgery, but once again, I relied on that confidence I had that originally brought me to this place in life. I also relied on the confidence my wife, Jennifer, had. Even though it wasn't an easy change for her either, she never wavered. She was so supportive. I think if she were feeling uncertain as well, we would have reconsidered things. Even though there were many days that I didn't feel equipped, somehow we made it all work. I found the resolve to stay true to my commitment to my family and to what I believed was a part of my calling, even during the uncertain times.

In 2006, I had another marked moment in my life. I was invited to attend the Billy Graham Library dedication, where I met a man named Dr. Dick Furman. He walked right up to me, introduced himself, and said, "I heard you are a surgeon and I want to talk to you." He proceeded to tell me all about World Medical Mission, a branch of the humanitarian aid organization, Samaritan's Purse, which was founded by Robert Pierce and Franklin Graham, son of the late Billy Graham. I was then invited to join a team of surgeons for a medical mission's trip overseas. It was the first time I had a break from the fire hose of growth and activity at our church, and I welcomed the opportunity to practice medicine again. I had been overseas before, but this trip changed me. Just as sure as I was about coming to help the church, I knew that this was the first step on a new path that my life was headed on.

Ever since that first trip over thirteen years ago, each year I spend four to five months in the remote regions of the world, where I relieve long-term missionary surgeons so they can return to their home countries to visit friends and family, and rest. On average, I perform hundreds of surgeries each trip, many of them lifesaving. My wife and children often come with me, and we serve the mission hospital together as a family.

It's pretty amazing what you see over there. Simple problems that we could treat so easily in the United States become big problems in these remote regions, because people have no access or limited access to medical care. One time, I was in a mission hospital in western Zambia near Angola, and after I finished three and half months of work there, one of the surgeons came up to me and said, "Do you realize you have been the only qualified surgeon in an area the size of the state of Louisiana?" The reality was sobering. My heart was so moved because once you've seen the needs of people, once you've seen the lack of medical care, once you've seen them die, you can't unsee that. It leaves a mark on your soul.

A few weeks later, I landed back in Houston, Texas, home of one of the largest medical centers in the world. In Houston, there are 2,500 physicians in one zip code. That's when Jennifer and I decided to launch our annual Mobilizing Medical Missions (M3) Conference. Our first one was in 2016, and it was out of a desire to connect the great needs of what we were seeing on the mission field with the great resources that we have in our own city, and really our country. We wanted to bring people together, to inspire them and help them connect with organizations so they can find their own mission and give back locally or globally. Each year, we partner with many local churches from different denominational backgrounds. We have about seventy-five humanitarian organizations and ministries join us as sponsors and exhibitors. Thousands of people have been inspired and challenged to discover their place in global missions, and Jennifer and I are so honored to help facilitate this effort. It's been a great beginning, and I know we will have an even greater impact as we grow in the future.

So often we've found that people are overwhelmed by need—and the need is incredible. But it was a paradigm shift for me personally to see that we can make a difference. Maybe we can't solve the whole problem, but we can do something to begin to solve the problem. We shouldn't look at the need and be paralyzed or overwhelmed. We should look at the need and say, "What do I have? What can I do?" That is what we strive to instill in people through M3.

When I look back over my life, I can see how each step has prepared me for the next, even when it didn't make sense at the time. It was all part of God's plan working together for a higher purpose. I could have stayed where I was in Arkansas and retired with a lot of money, but I know I would not be nearly as happy or feel fulfilled. Now at this stage in my life, I'm more content than I've ever been. For me, medical missions are the most rewarding, incredible experiences that I could ever have. It's pure soul satisfaction, knowing that my work is significant and that I am making a significant impact on the people I encounter. If I were to die tomorrow, I couldn't ask for another thing. My life has been absolutely incredible from the standpoint of what I get to do right now. But I am just in my early sixties, so I feel like I have a lot more to give and a lot more of life ahead of me.

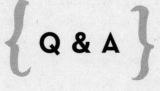

{ Q & A }

You said that you can see now how every step led you to where you are today. Hindsight is always 20/20, right? What advice would you give to your younger self, looking back?

That's simple. I would tell myself to relax, that it all works out. I would also say, work on your self-awareness . . . do the inner work to find out who you are. This work I'm doing would not be as satisfying if I wasn't self-aware.

What would you say to someone who is in transition but not sure about their next step?

Well, from my experience, I think one of the most important things you can do as you work out your purpose is to find out who you are—what drives you, what angers you, what gives you joy. That's what I mean by working on your self-awareness. Take time to do self-assessments and be willing to receive input from trusted friends.

When I was younger and in surgery, I had my head down. I was driven, but I was also filled with anger and disappointment from the past. These feelings were still driving me at age thirty-seven, and while that made me want to be a really good surgeon, it also limited me in my relationships. However, the more you understand yourself, the more understanding you can be with others. After years of self-work, I now approach my relationships in a totally different way. I'm a huge fan of tools like the Enneagram, the StrengthsFinder assessment, and understanding things like the Five Love Languages.

You know, another thing that came to mind . . . I focused heavily on math and science growing up pursuing my medical degree. I think if I would have engaged in the arts a little bit more, it would have softened me a bit. There's a lot of value in creative expression that asks you to be more emotionally aware, reflective, and connected. So while you are exploring different paths and opportunities, give yourself permission to be creative and "color outside the lines," so to speak. You never know what you will learn about yourself when you get out of your routine.

What was the most significant part about your inner self-work?

I would have to say having the awareness of my internal drivers. I became aware that, deep inside, subconscious forces in my life were affecting me in a negative way as a direct result of unforgiveness. Growing up, I had friction with my dad like most teen boys do. We just saw things differently. That friction kindled a fire inside of me. After I went through a difficult divorce, it added fodder to that fire. I had this furnace burning inside. As long as it was directed toward work or sports, it was fine, but it also burned other people.

At age thirty-seven, I went back to that place inside me where it all started at age seventeen and I forgave my dad and released every bit of anger and hurt. It was like someone just flipped a switch inside of me and turned off the furnace. That's when the transition really began. When I forgave.

I think all of us need to work through that process of forgiveness. We've all been hurt. Our families aren't perfect. Parents aren't perfect. Sometimes we hold on to hurts that weren't even intentional, or offenses that are based on wrong or immature perceptions. As we get older, we see things differently. Taking time to let go of the past through forgiveness does a world of good to lighten the load of life so you can have a fresh, clear perspective moving forward.

Another thing I became aware of is that I lean toward perfectionism. That's a great quality when you're a surgeon. No one ever wants someone cutting on them with a "close enough" mentality. However, I realized I was too hard on myself in other areas. I had to learn to forgive myself and receive grace for the areas where I fell short in life.

Developing this self-awareness has allowed me to be truer to myself. And being truer to myself makes me more comfortable, confident, and content. I'm a kinder, gentler parent, and a kinder person toward myself.

What perspective do you think has changed the most, now in your second act?

As I said, I was a bit of a hardhead in my younger years. I was a hard worker with strong opinions, and when I made a decision, there wasn't much room for discussion. But right around age fifty, I learned something, and I say it often when sharing my views and opinions. I will say, "I think I'm right, but I may be wrong." I am much more open now in my second half of life, and I am willing to admit it when I make a mistake. I hope I model that for my children.

PATTY's POINTS

● **Take time to test your feelings.**

When Paul shared with his friends that he was thinking of making such a drastic life change, leaving his medical practice to support his father's church, well-intentioned friends pushed back. Patients understandably were upset at losing not only their medical doctor but a trusted friend and counselor. Yet Paul kept going. How did he know he was doing the right thing? Well, he didn't rush into his decision. He initially questioned his feelings and gave himself time to see if those feelings changed. He asked his wife's advice, and she supported him. Then he heard the objections of trusted friends and patients. Still, his heart didn't move.

Strong desire is necessary when you are contemplating trying something new or making a big change. But it's good to test your feelings and desire as Paul did.

Notice that even after Paul made the move to Houston, he continued to question himself for the next two years. I, too, had many ups and downs during my nine years in New York. Despite moving there for acting, I rarely got to do any! Most of my time was spent working survival jobs and taking classes. Many times I wondered if I should move on to something else, but my desire was still strong. If despite difficulties and doubts your desire beckons you to move forward, that's a good indication you are where you need to be.

- **Do your self-work.**

I love how Paul's first advice to people in transition is to find out who you are and what drives you. I think it's so important to do self-assessments and to take counsel from trusted friends or even talk to a professional. I'm a huge fan of evaluations such as Myers-Briggs, DISC Assessment, and honestly, therapy. Therapy is simply a way to get to know yourself and understand how you think and what's influencing you. It's a way to find truth in your life when perhaps your views have been distorted by disappointment or pain. As a mom, I made it a mission when raising my boys to make sure that they saw therapy as something completely normal, like going to the dentist or doctor when you have a problem. Their father and I both have spent seasons in therapy together and individually. I wanted to take the stigma off of it for them, because there should be nothing shameful about it. It doesn't mean there's something wrong with you. It means you want to grow and learn about yourself.

When you are trying to figure out your next steps, it's going to be easier if you've been tracking your internal drivers. You will be much more equipped if you know yourself well. People who move into second acts are often people who take stock of their lives and are ready to discover their purpose and place in this world.

- **Engage with the arts.**

I also love Paul's encouragement to engage with the arts. I think his assessment was right on, and I've experienced this in my own life. Even though, as an actress, my entire world is immersed in the arts, I still look for ways to stretch myself creatively. Did you know that engaging with the arts raises your EQ, which is the measure of your emotional intelligence? Emotional intelligence is the ability to recognize, evaluate, and regulate your own emotions. It's the reason many therapists use art as therapy in their practice. It's emotionally grounding. Don't worry if you don't see yourself as an "artist" per se, that's not what's important. We all have a desire within us to create and to be creative, whether it is through an artistic expression, or creating a business plan for a new venture, or creating computer algorithms or creating solutions to solve the global health care crisis. Every career path requires some level of creative thinking and problem-solving, and by exploring the arts, you increase your capacity for it.

Exploring the arts doesn't mean you have to take a sculpting class, but you certainly can. It can mean going to a museum or the symphony and just getting around creative people. The important thing is that you get your brain out of the daily grind and allow your thoughts to color outside the lines of life!

REFLECTION QUESTIONS

1. Where do you see yourself in this story? What part of Paul's personality, character traits, or journey can you relate to or identify with?

   _____

   _____

   _____

2. What is your greatest takeaway from this story? List a lesson learned.

   _____

   _____

   _____

3. Do you find that uncertainty about your decisions becomes a roadblock for you, or are you able to move forward with resolve? If so, what can you do to make decisions from a place of certainty?

   _____

   _____

   _____

4. What are you doing to feed your creativity? List some things that you can do to stretch yourself in this area.

_____

_____

_____

A Whole New Vertical

The Second Act Story of Sarah Foley

Some stories of reinvention are not by choice—they aren't part of your plan. In fact, they aren't what you would ever imagine for your life. Sarah Foley was living life by design. She knew what she wanted and how to make it happen. Sarah was living what seemed like her perfect life, working as a spa director, when life took a tragic and unexpected turn. After a horrific accident, she was forced to re-define herself, reinvent her dreams, and reimagine her life. Now, as a paraplegic, Sarah's new "normal" is as a disability icon, advocate, life coach, and motivational speaker. Sarah first started working with the community of women with disabilities like her, but other women who weren't in wheelchairs started reaching out to her, saying, "I need to hear what you have to say. Don't leave me out." Sarah came to realize that we all have something that we need to overcome, something that could be a disability if we let it. She is now using her story to bring hope, inspiration, and empowerment everywhere she goes.

Here is Sarah's second act story.

Before the accident, life was pretty simple. As far as my career goes, things just seemed to always work out for me. I was born and raised in Utah, but I felt like I just didn't belong there. My dream growing up was to become an actress or television personality, but I knew I needed to have a way to pay the bills while pursuing that dream, so I became a massage therapist. I ended up getting recruited by a spa in Palm Springs, California, and while I was there, I landed a television hosting job. I was realizing my dream . . . but it was a temporary assignment. During that time, I recognized how much I actually enjoyed working with people in the spa world and decided to pursue something in spa management as the next step in my career. I was offered a spa manager and director position, of all places, right back in Utah. So life went full circle and I just sort of followed it. I started checking off boxes, so to speak, of the things I wanted to accomplish. I just felt like everything was headed in the right direction.

In September 2012, all of that changed. I was dating Sean, my boyfriend of six months, and we decided to go to southern Utah for the weekend with another couple, Cade and Kim, and our four dogs, my two and Sean's two. The first morning, Sean and I got up and took the dogs on a massive hike. It was a gorgeous morning. The air was clear, the leaves were changing, there was no one around, the scenery was breathtaking. We stopped to gaze out over the horizon at the large red rock formations and I looked at Sean and said, "My life is perfect. There just isn't one detail about any of it that I would change. I love my job, I have great friends and family, I'm totally in love, and everything right now is truly just perfect." We enjoyed that moment together and then headed back to meet up with Cade and Kim for breakfast.

A few hours later, we decided to go explore on ATVs. Cade worked in the business, so he was able to bring a trailer filled with all kinds of riding toys. We packed a picnic and planned an easy ride out for the afternoon to enjoy nature. I was the least experienced rider, so they gave me the largest of the machines knowing that it would be more stable and safer. The other couple got on their four-wheelers, and my boyfriend decided to ride a dirt bike. We headed out and found a trail that seemed to be a narrow fire access road. There was a path laid out, but it was basically a one-lane dirt road. At one point, the path went up and around a bend and we couldn't see what was on the other side. We weren't sure how far it went, so the two guys decided to go up ahead of us to make sure it was clear and safe for us girls. Kim and I stopped and waited, and after a few minutes, we looked up and saw Cade at the top of the hill waving at us to come along. We started moving forward around the bend, but what we didn't know was that Sean was headed back down the trail to get us. He had no idea that Cade had already signaled to us. I was riding in front of Kim and when I saw Sean's dirt bike pop out from around the corner, my inexperienced brain completely panicked because he was headed straight for me. All I could think was *I need to get off the trail!* Sean reacted first and pulled off to the side, and if I would have just gone straight it would have been fine, but that's not what happened. In my panicked state, I jerked the handlebars. I thought I was braking, but I was hitting the accelerator and gunning it. My front wheels hit the ditch and I just started flipping through the air, the seven-hundred-pound four-wheeler landing on my hundred-pound body with every roll. When I close my eyes I can remember it all very clearly. I tried to scream, but no sound came out. All I could hear was the crunching of my bones every time the four-wheeler landed on me. It rolled on me twice and then threw me up against a fallen tree. Finally, I landed, and everything became still. I was conscious and aware of how far I had been thrown by how long it took Sean to get to me. It's funny what goes through your mind at a time like this, but as I lay there waiting, I remember thinking of my second-grade teacher and a story she told us about a guy who had a motorcycle accident. She told us that when they moved him, it made the injury worse and killed him. So I kept thinking, *If I just don't move, I'll be fine.* As Sean approached, I yelled, "Call Life Flight, don't move me! How is my face?"

He just looked at me in shock.

"Your face is beautiful, but I have no idea about the rest of your body."

I had landed on my left side and my left clavicle was broken and causing me severe pain. The bone was ready to pierce through the skin. I still had my helmet on, thank God, but it was totally smashed. I haven't been able to bring myself to look at it, even to this day. I can't imagine what would have happened without it.

It took Life Flight about an hour and a half to get to me. When they arrived, the paramedics started evaluating me. Both of my shoes had been blown off, and when one of the paramedics started pinching my toes, I couldn't feel a thing.

They finally loaded me onto the helicopter, but no one else could come with me. I've never felt so alone in my life. They flew me to a hospital in Las Vegas because it was closer to where we were, even though it was farther away from home. I was immediately sedated and taken into surgery. I had nine broken ribs, snapped my clavicle, and crushed my spinal cord at T4, right around the middle of my back, so I was not able to feel a thing below that level. What's crazy is that with all my injuries, I did not have a scratch of blood, not even a carpet burn. Just crushed bones.

I was in surgery for ten hours and then woke up alone in my hospital room. I was completely disoriented with tubes coming out of me everywhere and machines beeping all around me. I felt like I couldn't breathe and started to panic. I began thrashing around trying to get up, but I couldn't get up. I couldn't make my legs work. That reality was overwhelming. Just then a nurse came running in. She tried to calm me down, saying, "Just breathe. Breathe normally. That's all you have to do right now." Which seemed like a massive task.

As the nurse calmed me down, she told me I had a waiting room full of people: Sean, my mom, my stepdad, my brother, grandpa, aunt, and three different girlfriends from three different states. I was still in the trauma unit, so they could only come in one at a time. Every one of them said that when they heard what happened, they dropped everything and just went on autopilot to get to me as fast as they could. Their blanket of love brought me comfort. My aunt Stacy is very close to me and she has always had a great impact on me throughout my life. When she came into my room she wrapped her arms around me, I just melted into her. I whispered in her ear, "Why?" She immediately pulled away and looked me in the eye sternly and said sharply, "Don't you *ever* ask why. That answer is going to come when it's supposed to come, not when you ask it. And it will eat you alive trying to figure it out."

Her words were sobering and have carried me during many difficult moments. Those words kept me from spiraling into the land of "why," which is a dark and barren place. She's right. You will never get the answer while you are asking for it. You just have to go through the journey of figuring it out and realize it's not always going to look the way you expect it to.

After the trauma unit, I was transferred to another intensive care unit for three weeks, and then I was flown to Craig Hospital in Colorado, which is the number one hospital in the nation for spinal cord injury. It's where Superman actor Christopher Reeve was sent after his horseback riding accident. In the helicopter on the way to Craig, I started having symptoms of a staph infection, and they determined that I contracted spinal meningitis from the Las Vegas hospital, which is a serious infection that can cause brain damage in a matter of hours and death within twenty-four hours if left untreated. By the time we dropped down in Colorado, I was beyond sick. They put me right back into the ICU and I don't remember a thing about the next ten days. I was borderline comatose the entire time, desperately fighting for my life. Once I was stable, I spent another three months at Craig in therapy, learning how to get dressed, go to the bathroom, navigate a kitchen, and other ways of independence to prepare me to go home. Unlike most spinal cord injury patients, I was never given the words "You'll never walk again." At one point, the doctors pulled my whole family into my room for a meeting. They also set up a speakerphone and arranged for extended family and friends to listen in. The doctor pulled up my X-rays and showed exactly what was happening in my back. The X-rays showed the broken bones, newly placed metal rods and pins, and my spinal cord. The prognosis was actually promising because my spinal cord had only been compressed against the bones but not severed in any way. They simply left it open as a wait and see, however I was advised to work the physical therapy as if no feeling or function would come back, although I didn't accept that possibility.

The rehabilitation program at Craig Hospital is amazing! In the basement of the building is a huge room filled with things like baby cribs, airplane seats, a kitchen, and even a car cut in half so you can relearn how to drive and practice normal daily life activities. They teach you how to transfer in and out of a car, and how to break down your wheelchair and store it piece by piece next to the driver's seat. In the beginning, that process took me about thirty minutes, and that was with help. Today, my time is within about forty-five seconds. They also have a driver's ed program right on-site. They take you in a car that is adapted with hand controls to an open parking lot to practice. It was super awkward at first. Not only did I have to learn how to use hand controls, but I had to learn how to keep from falling over when going around the turns. You don't think about how much your legs stabilize you when you drive until they don't. Eventually I got the hang of it and when I drove alone for the first time it was about as close to the joy of walking again—a taste of freedom.

I was always hopeful that I would regain use of my legs and it never occurred to me that I wouldn't walk out of Craig Hospital. The day I left, it was both a relief to be able to go home, but a hard pill of reality to swallow that I wasn't walking. In the spinal cord injury community, there is a belief that whatever comes back by the two-year mark is what you'll be set with for life. That's about the time that all swelling is gone, so it would be a long wait-and-see game.

At home, the road to recovery was just beginning, except it wasn't really a road to recovery; it was the road to coping with my new normal. First, I had to figure out what my new normal was. It was a long and lonely road, even when there were people around and worse when they weren't. When you are in the hospital, you are everyone's biggest priority. My family even put together a visitation calendar to ensure I was never alone. But after about five months of being at home, reality started to hit hard. I knew in my heart I would be okay, but I had no idea what okay would look like. Everyone else got to go back to their normal lives, doing normal things, working normal jobs, and driving normal cars. There was nothing normal for me and I was like, "Now what?" Nothing works anymore when you find yourself suddenly in a wheelchair. You can't even wash your hands in the sink the way you used to.

I finally got a new car and had hand controls installed. For the first few months it was like being fifteen again! My first road trip alone was to visit a friend about three hours away. My family was scared to death, but I desperately needed the freedom. Today I drive a convertible and, honestly, when I cruise with the top down, I completely forget I even have a disability. It's total bliss!

I also forced myself to get back to work running the spa as soon as I could, within seven months of the accident. The entire resort was so supportive, and I even came back to a completely remodeled office with wheelchair accessible features. I'm not sure if it was the best move to stress my body so much physically while I was still healing, but getting back to work did a lot for me emotionally. My job was like a bridge to the old me—who I missed so much. I was the boss and people relied on me, which was so empowering after being completely dependent on everyone else after the accident. But it wasn't "business as usual" by any stretch. As much as I needed to be there, it was also difficult for a very long time. Thank God for my staff! There were a few people who I could be super honest with when I needed help. I could tell them if I'd just peed my pants and ask them to ring me up some new ones from the spa boutique and bring them to me in the restroom so I could change. I could also be really honest with my boss when I needed to work from home because I was having extreme anxiety, which would come in waves.

I would put on a brave face all throughout the day, but then every evening as I would wheel myself to the elevator to go down to my car in the parking garage, I would feel the overwhelming tidal wave of emotion rising up. I would take a deep breath and hold it all in, but as soon as I would get into my car, load up my wheelchair, and close the door, the tears would erupt. I would just sob my entire forty-five-minute commute home. I would ask myself, *Why am I still here? What am I doing with my life now?* As big as my job felt to me before the accident, it felt very small after the accident.

Sean and I stayed together through all of this, and on the two-year anniversary of the accident, we were married and I was three months pregnant. It was all such bliss and at the same time I was still in so much denial. We both were. I didn't want a single wedding photo taken of me in my wheelchair. I didn't want to be defined by it and I was still hopeful I would get rid of it. But here I was at the two-year mark, and not much in my body had changed. I had one tiny spot on my right knee that I could feel and I struggled with accepting my fate in a wheelchair.

Six months later, I gave birth to our son, Charlie, which surprisingly was the easiest part of my whole journey. I woke up at 3:00 a.m. with a tight feeling in my upper abdomen. Sean turned the light on and noticed that my water broke, so he took me to the hospital, and within one hour Charlie was here with two simple pushes. It's amazing how the body just knows what to do. Because I couldn't feel anything, it was like I had a natural epidural and I was totally relaxed.

Becoming a mom in a wheelchair is something I never envisioned, and at the same time it's beyond what I could ask for. I fall in love with my son all over again every single day and he gives me a new sense of purpose and resolve.

Around the fourth year after the accident, Sean had a job transfer that took us to Maui, where I began an intense healing journey. I had to let go of my job at the spa, which I was holding on to simply because it was the last bit of normalcy I had. It was my last connection to the old me, to my life before the accident. Letting go of it was like letting go of who I used to be. It felt like a death.

I knew Hawaii would help frame up the new me, which I was looking forward to. The island of Maui is so healing with the gorgeous blue ocean, lush land, many natural practitioners, and a high focus on nutrition. Health is a huge part of the culture in Hawaii, and I fully immersed myself in it.

As time went on, I was fully focused on maximizing the usage of my body with the hope of one day walking again. It was intense and exhausting. I had been doing so much physical therapy trying to learn how to use my broken body that, one day, I was just tired of it all. I had gotten what's known as "wheelchair tummy" from not using my body fully, so I hired a personal trainer and I said to him, "I just want to look good in a bikini. I don't care about techniques to help me get in and out of my car anymore, I just want to feel good at the beach."

My trainer had never worked with anyone in a wheelchair and he was understandably nervous about it. But we worked together to develop a program that I could do. I dropped thirty pounds and got really fit. As I started posting my progress photos online, people started reaching out, saying, "How did you do that? Show me the way!" Now my trainer and I are business partners in developing personalized programs for people with or without disabilities.

Soon after, women from all over the world started contacting me about how to get rid of their "wheelchair tummies" and have the confidence to go after their dreams. This is what inspired my coaching and motivational speaking business, Vertical Blonde, based on the premise that being vertical isn't just about standing up, it's about a mind-set and an elevated way of looking at life. I host regular small-group events, and the transformation in the women is astounding. One woman said to me after one of my events, "Today I forgot I had a disability." She felt totally accepted, understood, and empowered, instead of defined by her limitations.

My reinvention was forced, but now I see it as the greatest blessing of my life. The person I've become in the process is a person I am proud of. Being able to inspire and encourage people is the greatest blessing. My life paints a symbolic picture that anyone can relate to, the wheelchair being the obstacle, and moving on with life by embracing it, the victory. I try my best to do it with grace and excitement, now knowing that on the other side of every struggle there is growth and blessing. It took my life being really, really messy to realize that perfect is unattainable. Instead, it's better to strive to find happiness within myself, and to make the person I am today a little bit better than I was yesterday.

{ Q & A }

You have a really amazing outlook on life, especially considering all that you've been through. How do you think your perspective has affected the quality of your life and general well-being?

Everything plays a role. You can get really distracted with how difficult things are. Working with people in the disability world, you see a lot of bitterness, anger, and sadness—things didn't go the way they wanted it to. But there are very few people who have the perspective where they realize they've been given a second chance. Most people with spinal cord injuries shouldn't be alive. Between the accident and then contracting spinal meningitis, I escaped death twice. It took me a while to get out of denial and get through the grieving process. It's so important that we travel through those stages at our own pace. But I think we can speed it along by changing our perspective and looking forward and saying, "Now what do I get to do?" So instead of asking, "Why me?" ask, "What can I do next with everything that has happened to me?"

How did you come to accept what happened and see it as a catalyst to your next season in life?

The more we stop resisting change and the more we embrace it, the more opportunities we will have to learn and grow. We have to have the perspective to say: "Actually, this may just be part of my calling, and this difficulty may be life's way of waking me up to that." We can go through struggles with grace if we are looking for the opportunity to grow and learn new and different ways of thinking and meeting new people.

But getting to the place of acceptance after a major tragedy or loss is a process. Grief is a process. Everyone goes through it differently and at their own pace. There's no right or wrong way to go through it. But for me, what I've learned to do now is to set my eyes on what I have to gain on the other side of my pain. When I face struggles I think, What am I going to learn now? How will this serve me in the future? *When I look for that growth, it keeps me moving forward past the difficulty.*

You talked about grieving your past and going through the process of letting it go. What was something that helped you the most in this process?

Oh my goodness, for sure therapy, and specifically an exercise my therapist had me do, which I will explain in a minute. I'm so grateful for her and all the people who have helped me on this journey. My friend said something profound to me one day: "Only we can heal ourselves, but we cannot do it alone." I would have never come this far without the people around me, or without asking for help and being willing to receive from those who care about me.

So one day, I went to see my therapist and I was furious. I was sitting there looking down at my hands. I had it. I had my perfect life in my hands. It was right here and then it was gone in the blink of an eye. Letting go of that perfect life was so hard, and I just grieved her—the old me. As I explained to my therapist how I was feeling, she looked at me and said, "You need to have a funeral for her." That was the craziest thing I'd ever heard, but that's exactly what we did.

I'll never forget leaving her office that day. I asked her, "How do I know when I'm done?"

"Done?" she asked.

"How do I know when I'm done processing all of this stuff from the accident? When will I be over it?"

"Sarah, there's a part of you that will never be over it and that's okay."

Her words hung with me, and then a wave of relief washed over me. There was no pressure to get to the finish line or check off a box or drive to find perfection again. There was nothing to run or hide from. Nothing to be labeled "undone." Only me in a wheelchair and the way I felt, and that was okay.

What are the top three things you would say to someone who is in a "forced" transition in life that they didn't plan for?

First, I would say, let go of why. The answers you need will come in due time. This was a huge revelation for me, and I'm so glad those words came to me from my aunt right in the beginning of my journey.

Second, I would say, be aware of your perspective and change it if needed because our reality is completely based on our perspective. When you embrace that notion, you realize how much control you have to change. Reality is a blend of filters through which we see life. These filters are made up of the way we were raised and what we've experienced—traumas, victories, events, people, books, movies, music, and more. All of these affect our perspective; however, most people rarely take the time to question any of it. Why do we view things the way we do?

The last person we tend to listen to is that voice deep within us that is buried under all of that other stuff. But the fastest way to feel joyful, free, and alive is to think, speak, and act from that voice within. The best tool I've found for letting that voice be heard is to journal. Allowing yourself to freely let the pen hit the paper and just write what's in your mind with no expectation is therapeutic and by far the best sleep medicine known to mankind. Over time, you will begin to uncover a person within you who you truly love. You will get a clear picture as to where your selfwork still needs to be done. If I've learned anything in my healing journey by journaling, it's that the more healing I've done, the more I realize I still have to do! And that's a beautiful thing!!

Finally, I would say, know that your greatest gifts are your struggles, because when we get past the struggle, we find new strength and we learn about who we are in a completely different way.

PATTY's POINTS

- **Focus on the positive.**

  Sarah's story is, of course, inspiring, but I had feelings of dread as I put myself in her place. I immediately thought of all the things I would have to change in my life if I had an accident like hers. I honestly don't know if I would be able to not only cope the way Sarah did, but to absolutely transform my life into such a positive and life-giving adventure! But as she says, it's both a process and a matter of perspective. The perspective part is very interesting to me. How many of us can't see the positive in our lives because of the perspective through which we have chosen to see ourselves and our situation?

- **Let go of what no longer serves you.**

  I loved the story of having a funeral for her old self, her old "perfect" life. There are probably things we could all let go of, accident or not, things we are holding on to that just don't or won't fit our life anymore. It has challenged me to look deeply and root out things I may be subconsciously holding on to that might actually be holding me back. I think it's important to take time to consider these things as we do our selfwork. Just as a tree drops leaves in the autumn season, we too need to let go of things in certain seasons so that new things can begin to grow in us.

● **Surround yourself with people who can see your future when you can't see it yourself.**

As with so many of these stories, Sarah credits those around her—her therapist, her trainer, her friends and family—with much of her successful transition. These people saw in Sarah what on many days she couldn't see herself. They believed in her and encouraged her to stay on the very difficult path she was walking through. I can't stress this enough: we cannot take these journeys by ourselves. We were created to live in a community, both for our general well-being, but in particular in times of tragedy. Having support in our lives is important even if we aren't contemplating a second act. But the folks around you need to be good listeners—no "Negative Nellies" allowed! Side note: Make sure you can tell the difference between a naysayer and someone who is pragmatic or has constructive criticism. Just because we don't *want* to hear something, doesn't mean we don't *need* to hear it!

● **Consider journaling.**

Journaling seemed to really help Sarah sort through her emotions, and honestly, it is something I have always resisted. I tried it once or twice many, many years ago, but when I would go back and read my thoughts, I would feel so embarrassed by them I'd rip the pages up! Since so many people benefit from this habit, maybe it's worth giving it another shot. (You try it first and let me know how it goes. ☺)

REFLECTION QUESTIONS

1. Where do you see yourself in this story? What part of Sarah's personality, character traits, or journey can you relate to or identify with?

    _____

    _____

    _____

2. What is your greatest takeaway from this story?

    _____

    _____

    _____

3. Have you found yourself slipping into a negative perspective by focusing more on what's wrong in your life than what's right? Take a moment to list the things that are good and positive in your world and focus on them. Maybe take a photo of your list and make it your phone home screen to keep it before your eyes.

    _____

    _____

    _____

4. Is there something from your past that you need to let go? Consider taking time to write a eulogy and say good-bye to it. Maybe it's a previous version of yourself, or a dream, idea, or relationship that didn't work out. Let go of the old so you can make room for the new.

_____

_____

_____

10

A Second Act Baked from a Second Chance

The Second Act Story of Dave Dahl

Thirty years ago, no one would have guessed that Dave Dahl would be a successful entrepreneur, public speaker, and philanthropist. Beginning in the 1980s he was addicted to drugs and in and out of prison. After completing his last sentence, in the mid-2000s, Dave returned to his family's bakery where he was inspired to create his own unique line of all-natural, organic breads called Dave's Killer Bread. He shared his story of transformation on the package along with his burly caricature on the label, a branding decision that attracted fans and massive media attention. Although he started humbly selling his loaves at the local farmers' market, demand and distribution rose over the years. Dave helped manage the growth of the business from twenty-five employees to nearly three hundred. By 2012, gross sales were $53 million a year, and the Dahl family eventually sold the business to Flower Foods for $275 million.

All of this would have been impressive for a Harvard business grad, but Dave was a high school dropout and ex-con with a mental illness, undiagnosed at the time. Now retired from baking, Dave is transitioning into his second act and following his passion to help others find hope, purpose, and meaningful careers, even if they've made mistakes in life like he did. He partners with humanitarian organizations and speaks in prisons, at businesses, and for various organizations, where he shares principles on how to find a new path and change the course of your life.

Here is Dave's second act story.

I was a four-time loser before I realized I was in the wrong game. Fifteen years in and out of prison is a hard way to find yourself.

My life got off course back when I was an insecure, pimple-faced teenager. My family owned a bakery, and I was expected to work there, but I wasn't sure what I wanted to do with my life and I often butted heads with my dad, as most teenage boys do. The kids in school started experimenting with drugs. Temptation was all around me.

The first time I got high on methamphetamines I felt empowered and confident, like I could do anything—and I liked that feeling. That first experience started me down a very destructive path that drove me to do anything to get a fix, things I'm not proud of. I spent fifteen years of the following two decades in prison on drug and robbery charges.

In 2001, while serving my time, I was placed on a drug treatment program and received vocational training in computer-aided drafting and design. I was also treated for depression, and the medication I was prescribed helped me get out of the negative headspace I was in. A lot was changing inside of me during this time. Using my mind in a creative capacity, and seeing what I could produce, gave me a completely different perspective on my life. I felt empowered in a new way, a healthy way. I excelled in the drafting course and started teaching other inmates the trade. When I was released in 2004, I felt more content with myself. I was ready to go back to work in the family bakery.

Using the creativity I tapped into while learning drafting, I came up with my own bread recipes that appealed to a wider demo and called it Dave's Killer Bread. Over the following decade, the popularity of the bread exploded. It started in the local farmers' market and ended up in stores nationwide with sales exceeding $50 million a year. It was a success that no one could have predicted. My face was the face of the brand, and no matter how hard I tried to maintain my humility, I became a parody of myself because I was the brand for the company. The business became my whole life. So when we sold Dave's Killer Bread in 2015, it felt like everything good I had worked for, everything that represented the new me, was gone. I had to "let my baby go," so to speak, and deep down I wasn't really ready for that. The stress of what was happening at this stage of life was beyond what I could handle. I had a complete mental breakdown and it wasn't pretty.

After the breakdown, they ran some tests and determined that I had bipolar disorder. On one hand, I was somewhat relieved to have some answers, but I also grieved over all the people I had hurt because of it. It took me a good three years to get past it. At first, I wasn't sure how to find my footing again, but I knew I had to stage another comeback for myself, like I had done before.

The first step was finding humility again and asking for help. A lot of people think humility is weakness, but that's not true. Humility is really a strength. Once we find humility, we become teachable. Being teachable means we can learn, and learning is power. So I had to become humble again. I had to stop worrying what others thought about me. I also knew I needed to distract myself creatively, like I had when I immersed myself in drafting all those years earlier, and subsequently in my breads. This time I chose African art. I became a collector and opened a showroom in Clackamas, Oregon, and then a boutique in Portland's Pearl District. Proceeds went toward feeding initiatives in Africa. People ask me all the time why I chose African art. Honestly, because it had nothing to do with the life of Dave Dahl, and that's what I needed—something completely outside of myself. I first became interested when I was at a concert, of all places. I was standing in line waiting to go in and on the wall of the building was a great big African mask. It grabbed my attention and I wanted to get one. My love for African art was born.

It took me a few years to find my new rhythm in life and start contributing back to the community again. As I came through this difficult transition in my life, I became aware that the principles I applied were the same as what brought me out of my destructive cycle in prison. What I learned in the process of helping myself, I could also teach to others. So that's what I'm doing now through partnerships and public speaking. My passion is to help people get back on track in life. I want to see others find fulfillment in meaningful careers the way I did. That's part of the legacy I left at Dave's Killer Bread, where 30 percent of their employees are ex-cons. Now I work with organizations that have related missions, to help people get back on track in life.

I'm a big part of an organization called Constructing Hope that was started in 2005 by an African American pastor. It's helping so many people. It's a six-week apprenticeship that teaches the construction trade but also provides services to help people in other areas of their lives, too. I work with a variety of organizations that help with things like housing, vocation training, job placement, and more. I like to consider myself "the hub." I'm good at making connections that solve problems for people. The right opportunity changed my life, and opportunity is a huge key to helping people make a turnaround.

The other thing I get excited about is helping people see that no matter what circumstance they are in, they can be successful, because success starts in the mind. Your mind is the starting point of resiliency, which is the ability to get back up after you've been knocked down, or after you've fallen down. It's the ability to keep trying even when things aren't working out the way you had hoped. Resiliency is also about humility and acceptance, and if you discover those things, it will give you the courage to come back from anything. I believe that resiliency is the forerunner to success.

I also tell people, sometimes if your brain isn't cooperating, medication might be the thing to help. It's what I needed, and it's nothing to be ashamed of, so talk to your doctor about it. We shouldn't be ashamed to get the help we need and use the resources available to us to become our best, whether its medication or therapy, diet, exercise, vocational training, or all of it. I'm living proof that even if you have a rough start at life, even when you've made bad choices, or did things you regret, even when you have a mental imbalance, you can have a wildly successful life. It's not where you start, it's whether or not you are moving forward on this journey of life. We have to see the value in the struggle and learn to embrace failure so we can get past it. Failure is a huge part of learning and growing and so we can learn to appreciate the value in it. When we get past the struggle, we find strength and it reinforces who we are.

I'm fortunate that I've struggled so much because I can really appreciate every moment that much more. I've been through a lot. My message is: If I can have success in the second half of my life, if I can impact others, anyone can. Change is an option for everyone, and it starts with hope, humility, and resiliency. Then you set your mind in the direction you want to go.

{ Q & A }

You started hiring ex-cons when you were running the bakery. A lot of businesses would see that as a risky decision. What was your thought process behind that?

Yeah, we became known for employing and helping ex-cons. It kind of just happened. We were interviewing and if a candidate seemed a right fit, we didn't hold it against them if they had a record. Then word got out because most ex-cons are turned down for jobs, and that often sends them right back to the streets. I got a second chance and it changed my life, so we believed in giving second chances. We wouldn't just hire anyone, we had to see that they were ready for a change, and when people are ready, it's the right thing to do to give them an opportunity. If someone needs an opportunity and you have one to give, you should give it. Thirty percent of our employees were ex-cons and we were hugely successful! That ought to tell you something about the value of giving people second chances.

You said that immersing your mind into creativity helped "distract" you from yourself. Can you tell more about that and do you recommend this for all people wanting to make a change?

When I was coming back from my mental breakdown, I just knew that some sort of hobby would be good for me. I had already experienced the grounding effect of doing something creative, and I knew I needed to get outside of my world since it felt like it was such a mess. So, yes, I would recommend doing something creative during a transition because creativity causes you to think outside the box. It can help you see things differently and broaden your perspective. For me, African art was more than a hobby because it was supporting programs to feed the impoverished in Africa, so it was a way I could give back after I had received so much. Doing acts of service and giving back is another way to balance your perspective.

What is the message you share when you are doing public speaking or sharing in prisons?

It's different each time because each group is so different. I leave a lot of room for questions. I start with a brief video and share my story. I talk about how grateful I am, and how I try to be accepting and humble, while at the same time striving for excellence in everything I do. Once we learn the power of acceptance and humility, we're surprisingly powerful.

I talk about forgiveness, too. The more we can forgive others, the more room we have in our minds to heal. If we heal, we can move forward. Holding on to negative thoughts keeps us from being the best we can be. I try to communicate that this journey isn't about being perfect, it's about constantly striving to be a better person. I tell them, "You're going to struggle, but remember that it's going to be okay. You're going to survive and be better than you were before." In the early days, I didn't think much of myself. I didn't know if there was hope for me. So I try to reassure people that as long as you keep trying, you are going to get there. Just be yourself. It's okay to be where you are at.

I realize that not everyone is able to go into a family business like I did, but I try to help them see where opportunity lies in their own circle. Then I open the floor for questions and try to get to the bottom of what their challenges are. My goal is to help them find hope because it's there for everyone.

PATTY's POINTS

● **Look for opportunity, even in the difficult moments.**

Dave's story is truly impressive. He's really on his third act, which is quite an accomplishment, given where he began. His path was extraordinary in both its difficulties and its triumphs.

Like many stories in this book, Dave's transformation unfolded in response to extreme moments. His time in prison is when he learned not only a trade—computer drafting—but it was then he also realized he needed help with his depression. Perhaps his success wouldn't have happened if not for his incarceration. Of course, it's easy to say that in hindsight, but his story is encouragement for any reader who feels overwhelmed by their circumstances. These difficult moments, if we view them as opportunities, can be a catalyst to look at ourselves honestly and make decisions that will lead to growth.

● **Take time to invest in your mental well-being.**

I'd also like to underscore the importance of mental health in Dave's story. Dealing with his depression enabled him to succeed in the drafting program, which in turn boosted his self-esteem. The transformation into a more confident and happier person paved the way for Dave to be able to successfully transition into an entrepreneur. But there was even more to come for Dave, just when it looked like he was on top of the world. With the wildly successful sale of his company, Dave realized the extent to which his intense work schedule was masking his bipolar disorder.

There's no doubt that we all have seasons of intense focus, work, or obligation, but we also need to take a break, to rest, reflect, and rejuvenate. I love that Dave's next baby step was to pursue creativity again. Engaging with the arts helps our mental well-being in so many ways.

● See yourself as a work in progress.

I like that Dave always circles back to work on himself. He seems particularly open to looking at himself and trying to change those things that are harming him and others around him. This ability has helped him to continually grow. I love that he's now sharing his struggles with others in the same situation.

The truth is, none of us ever really "arrive." We are each a work in progress, and when we embrace this truth, it really takes the pressure off. We can't be perfect, even though, now more than ever, we feel pressure to put our best foot forward—and filter and post a photo of us doing so. But we are all going to mess up at some point. We're going to make the wrong decision, say the wrong thing, hurt someone we love. We have to give ourselves permission to grow, to get back up when we fall, to keep moving forward. This is the work we all have in this life.

We can't expect perfection out of others any more than we can expect perfection out of ourselves. We'll be a lot less disappointed in other people when we view them as a work in progress, too.

REFLECTION QUESTIONS

1. Where do you see yourself in this story? What part of Dave's personality, character traits, or journey can you relate to or identify with?

_____

_____

_____

2. What is your greatest takeaway from this story?

_____

_____

_____

3. Everyone makes mistakes. Is there something in your past that is still affecting you in some way today? If emotions still rise up when you think about it, that's a good indicator that something inside needs healing. Can you make the decision to forgive yourself?

_____

_____

_____

4. We all need a break from the daily pressures of life. What are you
    doing to invest in your mental well-being? Do you make time to
    rest, rejuvenate, and enjoy recreation?

    _____

    _____

    _____

11

From Home Security to Relationship Security

The Second Act Story of Jim and Elizabeth Carroll

Jim Carroll has an eclectic background as an entrepreneur, inventor, author, poker champion, bounty hunter (yes, really!), and private investigator. He also runs a security company with more than two thousand employees nationwide. At first glance, you probably wouldn't guess that he has been revolutionizing marriages for more than thirty years, too. The Marriage Boot Camp Seminar was a by-product of his own search for inner healing. He felt driven to help others build successful and fulfilling marriages, even though his own had fallen apart. Finally, he had his own "happily ever after" when he met Elizabeth. She had a background in counseling psychology and together they grew the program. Soon, they began working with celebrity couples, which opened the door to host their own reality television show based on the seminar.

The chemistry between Jim and Elizabeth is undeniable, and their ability to work as a team to help others is a unique gift that has gained worldwide attention.

Here is Jim's second act story.

My childhood was laced with dysfunction and abuse. On top of that, I had survived horrific sexual abuse from outside my family. In my high school years, I became depressed and ended up spending a lot of time largely isolated from others. I had some deep wounds from early in my life that were affecting me as an adult, and I didn't even realize it.

One night, I started a journey of inner healing in a rather unusual way. An officer pulled me over for speeding. I was in my truck, on the side of the road, right in front of an old church. After the officer left, I got out of my car and walked into the church, feeling destitute. I ended up spending the night there, and in the quiet, peaceful setting I did a lot of soul-searching. Something changed in me that night and for the first time, I saw hope for my future.

As I moved into adulthood, I developed some close friendships, which helped me continue to grow and heal from my difficult childhood, but I still had a lot of work to do. In 1986, I attended a Dr. Phil seminar that catapulted me light-years ahead of where I had been in my healing journey. That seminar changed my life and I was grateful. By this time, I had been unhappily married for many years, and anger and hurt had become a way of life. I wanted my marriage to change, but I didn't have any relationship skills or tools to make that change happen. I was failing miserably in this area, but Dr. Phil broke through the shell of my anger and hurt and enabled me to open up again. I was so moved by the event that I trained under Dr. Phil for many years and continued to grow as a person, while learning how to coach others through the healing process as well.

Dr. Phil's seminar was pretty costly to attend, and I had the desire to develop something that could be more accessible to a wider range of people. I could see how everyone could benefit from this program. In 1994, with Dr. Phil's blessing and encouragement, I developed my own personal-enrichment seminar based on his principles and curriculum, but at a much lower cost to attend. I launched it as a nonprofit so that people could make donations to offset the costs for others or even sponsor a friend or a loved one. I also added an optional spiritual component for people who want to explore their faith or overcome hurts and disappointments from religious organizations.

When it came time to hold my first seminar, I didn't know what to expect or even how many people would attend. I knew in my heart if I didn't have at least thirteen people, I wasn't going to keep putting the time and effort into it. Sure enough, exactly thirteen people attended and they all had life-transforming experiences!

The program evolved over time and got better and better, growing mostly through word of mouth. About a decade later, I got a phone call from someone at TLC. They heard about the program, but they were looking for something they could base a reality show on that would help married couples. As it was, the program was designed as an individual experience, but it would still have a huge impact on relationships. Their request gave me an idea and that's when I revised the curriculum and tailored it to couples working both individually and together. The Marriage Boot Camp was born—an interactive event using games, drills, visualizations, and exercises to break down emotional walls and enhance the relationship between spouses or engaged couples. My own marriage had dissolved by then, but I was determined to do everything in my power to help others have successful marriages, and hopefully have one of my own someday, too.

TLC came and shot a pilot with the Marriage Boot Camp. Although it was the highest-rated pilot in TLC history, they decided to abandon the program because it was considered too intense for their network. But that didn't stop our momentum one bit. Every single seminar, we had stories of marriages restored, improved, connections rebuilt, forgiveness, and life-changing transformations that fueled my resolve and the resolve of my team.

But the greatest change to the program, and in my life personally, was in 2009 when I met and married Elizabeth, who happened to have a psychology degree, even though her background and career was in corporate sales. When we got married, Elizabeth joined me in running the bootcamp full-time, and not only did she have a second

act in her career, we both had another chance at the love we'd always
dreamed of.

Here is Elizabeth's second act story.

Before meeting Jim, I spent nearly thirty years in the corporate world
and went through a devastating divorce, my second one. I realized I
didn't know the man I had been married to for almost thirteen years.
After the divorce, I spent several years trying to make sense of the
pieces of my broken world. I had no idea how I would recover or how
I would start all over again at age fifty. I had a psychology degree that
I always hoped to do something with, but I was never sure what. People and relationships fascinated me, largely because of my experiences
growing up. My interest in psychology started way back when I was
just a little girl.

I was born and raised in Griffith, Indiana, a steel mill town at
the crossroads between Gary, Indiana, and Chicago. They call this area
"the black belt" because of the smokestacks and the racial mix. My
parents are interracial. They didn't even speak the same language when
they married. Not at all. My mom is Japanese and she couldn't speak a
word of English when she married my dad, who is a typical American
"mutt"—Welsh, Irish, and American Indian. He was in the service and
stationed in Japan during the Korean War, and that's where they met.
As an adult, I asked my mom why she would do such a thing and she
told me, "Your dad represented the American dream." We often take
for granted the freedoms we enjoy in this country, but she would do
anything for the opportunities we have here—even marry someone
she couldn't communicate with. You see, my mom was the firstborn in
her Japanese family. At that time, it was a dishonor to have a firstborn
girl and not a boy. In Japan, they were still doing ritual drownings of
firstborn girls, so my mother is fortunate to be alive. She lived because
a family member who couldn't have children took her in. My grandparents passed my mom off and tried again for a boy, and then had

five. My mom was raised with so much shame for being who she was. She felt unworthy and unwanted because of what happened. So naturally, she took her first ticket out of the country—my dad.

My dad was born to a fifteen-year-old, unwed mother. In the 1930s, that was a really big deal, so he grew up with a lot of shame as well. To say that neither one of them were equipped for a healthy marriage is a gross understatement! When my mom came to America, she had great dreams and high expectations based on what she heard about this country. She was ready for America, but she wasn't quite ready for Griffith, Indiana. And when she learned English, she did not stop talking—and my dad wasn't quite ready for that. So growing up, all I knew about marriage was that it meant two people fighting all the time.

So I essentially became my mother's therapist at age fourteen, and this is where my interest in relationship psychology first started. I wanted her to be happy, and I thought I could help. I would study my parent's relationship and look for ways to help them both communicate better. At the same time, I also had a dream of getting out of Griffith. I knew education was the key to bettering myself, so after high school, I took off to Indiana University and worked my way through.

I didn't realize how my parents' guilt and shame lived on in me, but I began to do some soul-searching after college when I recognized some pretty big insecurities in my life. I had been dating a guy who previously dated a woman named Margie Wallace. Now, Margie Wallace was a tall, blond actress and beauty queen—the first American to win Miss World in 1973. I wasn't any of those things; in fact, I was the exact opposite, so I would constantly compare myself to her and wonder if I measured up in my boyfriend's mind or anyone else's. One day, something inside me rose up and I thought, *Why are you letting this woman who you don't even know own you and occupy so much of your headspace?* As I thought about it, I realized it was really absurd. I began a quest to understand what was driving me and started reading every self-help book on the market with the goal of getting Margie Wallace out of my head. As I was learning about psychology and human behavior, I found all of the information so fascinating. And it worked. I got rid of Margie Wallace, and then I got rid of her ex-boyfriend.

Largely based on that experience, I ended up going back to school to get my psychology degree, simply because human behavior was all so interesting to me. I couldn't imagine how I would ever use my degree; I mostly wanted the information to help myself.

By this time, I had been working in sales and marketing, managing large corporate accounts for Levi Strauss & Co. in Chicago. My career was solid, but marriage was always one of my big dreams—one that I was still ill-equipped for. I was married and divorced in my late twenties and then married again in my late thirties, and this time I thought it would be forever. I had a daughter from a previous relationship, and then my second husband and I had a daughter together. From the outside, our family looked perfect, and nothing could have prepared me for what I learned after thirteen years of marriage.

My job with Levi brought us to Frisco, Texas, by way of Los Angeles and San Francisco. I was nearly fifty years old, and the girls were in high school and college when our world came crashing down. I found out something horrible about my husband. I was beyond devastated. I didn't even know the man I was married to. I immediately filed for divorce to protect my daughters. I went through a couple of years of deep depression. On top of the emotional trauma to my family, how in the world was I supposed to start all over again at age fifty? What would become of my dreams? I became determined to work hard the rest of my life, put my daughters through college, and accept my new reality. The only other option was to fall into a pit of despair, and I fought hard to stay out of it.

Several years later, I found my new rhythm and some women in the office encouraged me to start online dating. I wasn't thrilled about the idea, but I felt ready to get back out there, so out of curiosity I set up an online profile. After weeks of total disappointment, lo and behold, a match came to me that seemed reasonable. This guy was handsome with steely blue eyes, very interesting, and well put together. I reached out and gave him my number. About five minutes later, I got a phone call.

"Hello," I said.

"Take your number off my profile, immediately!" the voice said.

"Excuse me? Is this Jim?" I asked.

"Yes, you posted your number publicly on my wall, so anyone can see it. Do you know how many creeps are going to be calling you? Take it down immediately!" Jim said emphatically. Mr. Security was in full force.

"Oh, I didn't realize it was posted publicly. I'll take it down," I said.

"And can you meet me for dinner in twenty minutes?" Jim asked.

I was a bit surprised, but charmed by his unconventional opener.

"Sure. That sounds great."

And about twenty minutes later, I met Jim Carroll on a blind date. We had a wonderful time and connected right away. We both had such similar passions for helping people. After that night, we were practically inseparable, and we were married three months later in June 2009. The pieces of my world were coming together and forming a beautiful new picture. I could have a great love in marriage, I could pursue my passion in marriage counseling, and I could be home with my daughters—all things that were very important to me. In 2011, I formally retired from Levi after thirty years and poured my heart and soul into my second act with Jim and the Marriage Boot Camp.

What makes the Marriage Boot Camp different from every other program out there is that it's highly interactive with drills, games, and activities that help you identify and deal with behaviors or thought patterns that are not serving you.

The state of many marriages today is compromised by the fact that so many of us come from dysfunctional families. Nobody is really getting training in their family of origin on what healthy relationships look like. Everyone has wounds in some way, and then they start playing out those wounds when they start dating and get married. The problem is that you don't recognize what's happening unless the awareness is brought to the conscious mind.

A lot of marriage seminars have great information, but they spend most of the time teaching and lecturing and appealing to the intellect. In the Marriage Boot Camp, instead of spending thirty or forty minutes addressing the intellect, we spend no more than five minutes teaching, and then we follow it up immediately with an activity on how you apply that teaching to your life. We support that application by using a lot of tools to get into nonconscious places of the psyche, through guided visualizations and the use of music and stories. These activities tap into the left brain, where the emotion, creativity, and nonconscious files are stored. And when you unpack those places, you see what drives your behavior and how to change it. You see where your unresolved issues are so you can begin to resolve them. A person can listen all day long to lectures filled with really good information about what to do, but if there's nonconscious, unfinished business inside, you will sabotage yourself every single time and never know why.

There are several components to the curriculum and the first addresses "Who am I?" A lot of drills are designed to parse through your identity so you can get in touch with your inner drives and motivations. The second component is "Who are you?" meaning who is the person you are married to. A huge piece of the wholeness journey is understanding that your spouse has a completely different reality than you do, and that shapes their approach and understanding about life. So finally, you need tools on how to grow and heal coming from those two completely different arenas.

As Jim and I began to work together and revise the program as a couple, we also had to go through this process of healing and learning to grow together in our marriage, too. As you can imagine from our backgrounds, we had a lot of baggage between us, so we had to use our own tools to work through it, and we developed new tools in the process.

One of the drills that came out of our own conflict is called "Hot Buttons." This is an exercise that helps you understand the deeper wounding that causes us to overreact. When a reaction to something is elevated, that's a good clue that there is some unresolved hurt from the past related to this area. When you can connect the dots to the past, you can process the early trauma and take the power out of the present reaction.

I mentioned earlier my insecurity about blond, blue-eyed, fair-skinned women. Well, anytime my husband would notice a tall, beautiful blonde, I would hit the roof. Now I know enough to know that I was overreacting, but I didn't seem to be able to stop! We tried to get Jim to change some of his behavior, but trying to stop a man from noticing beautiful women is like trying to stand in a hammock. Not only was this unfair, it was impossible. I knew I had to deal with this insecurity. Then one day a memory came to me. When I was six or seven years old, there were a bunch of neighborhood boys that would taunt me and call me racist names because of my dark skin. One day at school, this group of boys started taunting me and pushed me down on the playground. It was icy and cold out and I slipped and hit my head. I woke up to find myself in bed and discovered that I had gotten a concussion from the fall. Without being aware, I developed a negative self-image from this and believed that I was inferior because of my skin color. Over time, this morphed into an adult "hot button," and when I compare myself to a fair-skinned blonde, I overreact. Once I made the connection, I could process that hurt as an adult and release Jim from paying for what the bullies did to me at seven years old.

Working together over the last decade hasn't always been easy. However, we've become better at what we do because we have walked through the process together and the insight we now have to help other couples is exponentially stronger. We've seen great success with our methods and spent time hosting our own reality show.

It all started in 2011, when ThinkFactory Media called us to ask us to work with Gene Simmons and Shannon Tweed, who were experiencing relationship issues; the wedding they had planned was in jeopardy. We worked with them on air and they went on to a happy, successful marriage. Then in 2012, we became Dr. Drew's Lifechangers when we were called to save the marriages of four of the most challenging couples. Again, they all had dramatic turnarounds. After that, ThinkFactory and WE TV wanted us to work with Bridezillas and their spouses, in a reality house. The show was a big hit and we were invited to appear on Fox News, the Kathie Lee show, CNN, *Fox & Friends*, Headline News, ABC, CBS, NBC, *Huff Post Live*, Arthur Kade, *Glamour* magazine, and more. After that, we hosted and produced the TV series *Marriage Boot Camp: Reality Stars*, which despite airing on Friday night, was one of WE TV's top shows. The series was a success for seven seasons.

Today, we are living the life we always dreamed of and still find our greatest joy in bringing hope and healing to relationships via the Marriage Boot Camp Seminars.

{ Q & A }

What encouragement would you give to someone who is experiencing a broken relationship like yours, who is maybe hoping for a second chance at love later in life?

Elizabeth: Through my journey, I learned that contentment is a choice. I became determined that no matter what life threw at me, I was going to be content. So day by day, I would say, "I choose to be content, even if I'm not happy, I'm going to be content and grateful." As I set my focus on contentment, it blossomed into a lifestyle of gratitude—because you can't be content without being grateful. That's when the bitterness started to disappear, and things in my life started changing. That's when I met Jim. I don't think Jim and I would have clicked if I would have met him as a depressed, bitter, and angry woman with a chip on my shoulder. It took a three-year journey of inner healing for me to reach the point of saying, "I am the author of my life. I get to choose my attitude. I may not be able to choose my circumstances, but I'm going to choose contentment."

Having said that, if I were giving someone advice during a difficult transition, I would say, do your grief work. It's really important to absolutely sink into all five stages of grief: denial, anger, bargaining, depression, and acceptance. And don't rush through to acceptance. But once you get to acceptance, live there and don't allow yourself to go back to being bitter and angry the rest of your life. Anger and bitterness are not attractive qualities. We can't expect the next spouse to heal us or to make up for what the previous one did. We each have to do our own self-work, and then when we meet someone, we can offer our strength, hopes, and dreams to the relationship. That's not to say there won't be baggage from both of you in the new relationship and plenty of work to do as a couple, but you have to take the responsibility and initiative to do your own grief work and selfwork.

What was your greatest opposition to making this shift? Was it internal or external?

Elizabeth: Both. The internal opposition was the temptation to fall into the pit of despair. It's true: misery loves company. There are a lot of sad, lonely, depressed people who love company, and they unknowingly try to keep you in the pit with them. It's hard work to climb out and it takes a conscious effort to stay out.

The other obstacle, a major external obstacle, was financial. Here I was a single mom and my ex had stolen so much money from me. He didn't work, and when we separated, he would do things like use my credit card to buy appliances for other people. I was broke, so I had to figure out how to make life work. Financial pressures alone can put you in a pit in a hurry, so those two things were really working against me. It took a daily decision to get beyond my feelings and do what I needed to do to take the next step in life.

What is something you gave up that you thought you never would?

Elizabeth: As part of my healing journey, I surrendered the notion of being married. In fact, I surrendered all of my dreams. That was a really big deal for me because I had a boyfriend constantly from the time I was fourteen years old. That was my lifestyle. More than that, it became a part of my identity. It gave me a false sense of confidence and security. During that season of transition, I determined that I could live life as a single mother. I didn't need a man to be okay, I was enough all on my own. I don't think that's a part of everyone's journey, but if your dream is the sole source of your happiness and confidence, it may be time to look at your life and make the choice that you can find fulfillment from within.

PATTY's POINTS

- **There's always a path to healing.**

Jim and Elizabeth's story is a great example of how the painful experiences of our lives can end up being what makes us successful
human beings, and can be used to teach others by sharing what we
have learned. Their personal stories are so encouraging, because
despite suffering abuse at the hands of others, they were able to
find their way through and out of their suffering into healing.
And that healing can come through unusual circumstances, like
Jim's "dark night of the soul" in an empty church. We never know
when or where God will speak to our souls. Jim also found mentors along the way that he could lean on.

Even in the difficult season of life, we have to remember,
there's always a way out, there's always a path to healing. Very
often, the path to healing can lead to a second act.

- **Be aware of what you allow to define you.**

Elizabeth had to learn a different lesson in order to heal. She states
that being in a relationship had been her identity since she was a
teen. Perhaps it was the need to be validated by a man that kept
her blinded to the dysfunction in her second marriage. She had to
learn independence, and see that she couldn't use marriage to save
her or define her.

We have to be careful about what we let define us. In the beginning of this book, I talked about surrendering my desire to act
and not letting it define me. How do you know if something or

someone is defining you? Imagine if that thing or person left your life. How would that affect you? Would you fall apart? Would you pick yourself back up?

Be open to trust again.

Both Jim and Elizabeth needed to learn to trust again, which can be very difficult when the people closest to you are the ones who betrayed you. Trust is vital to relationships and relationships are vital to success, whether a marriage partner, business partner, family relationship, or coworker. We have to examine how we approach people and make sure we aren't making them pay for our past pain.

I love the fact that Jim's and Elizabeth's individual journeys made them perfect partners in their own marriage and in helping others' marriages. Like Jamie Kern Lima and her husband, Jim and Elizabeth became partners in life and business. For some couples, working together can be a disaster. But in these instances, they were all able to stay together. I like that the stories in this book illustrate all kinds of paths and partnerships as you find your way to a second act—there's no right or wrong way to do it—just your way!

REFLECTION QUESTIONS

1. Where do you see yourself in this story? What part of Jim's or Elizabeth's personality, character traits, or journey can you relate to or identify with?

    _____

    _____

    _____

2. What is your greatest takeaway from this story?

    _____

    _____

    _____

3. Elizabeth talked about "hot buttons" as being something that triggers you to an elevated or exaggerated response. Can you recognize any hot buttons in your life and draw the connection to a wound from childhood that you need to process and release?

    _____

    _____

    _____

12

Laughing Last, Laughing Loudest

The Second Act Story of Dani Klein Modisett

Writer-comedian Dani Klein Modisett has been performing comedy for over twenty years. She taught the art of stand-up comedy at UCLA for over a decade and has produced numerous live comedy shows all over the US. Her work has addressed some of the biggest changes in a person's life and how humor can help you weather them. But when Alzheimer's disease befell her mother unexpectedly, she discovered an unconventional way to use laughter to ease difficulty and bring measures of healing. Her simple idea has garnered national exposure via media outlets such as the *Washington Post, Dr. Oz,* CBS News, and *The Doctors.*

Here is Dani's second act story.

I've been an actor and a comic for twenty-five years, starting in New York City and eventually immigrating to Los Angeles. Like most comics, I get material for my work from my life experiences. I also get inspired by other people's experiences, which led me to produce two live storytelling shows, the first of which was called *AfterBirth . . . Stories You Won't Read in a Parenting Magazine*. I rounded up funny friends to tell their stories about how becoming parents changed them unexpectedly and forever. The second show took on the subject of long-term marriage, specifically how to do it joyfully. This show was called *Not What I Signed Up For* and featured a comical spin on stories about some of the toughest aspects of marriage. Yes, you can live to laugh about it!

I loved helping people craft monologues about how these family experiences changed them. I rented out a club and produced live storytelling nights, which were terrific! The stories were hilarious and heartbreaking, and we had men and women from all aspects of the entertainment industry participating.

Later, *AfterBirth* became a book, followed by *Take My Spouse, Please*, which explored how laughter can help keep a marriage happy and healthy. Laughter seemed to be what helped people through life's toughest moments, so as I started a new chapter when my mother developed Alzheimer's, I turned to what I knew best, the thing I knew would get us through, finding a way to connect through laughter.

I'll never forget the day I got the call. My mother had always been extremely independent and was living in New York City, her hometown from birth. She was a corporate executive, buttoned up and put together, but suddenly all the wheels were coming off the bus. She was moody and couldn't manage simple tasks like filling out a bank deposit slip. She was behaving in ways that were completely unfamiliar to my mother's friends, my sister, and me. All signs pointed to Alzheimer's.

Since she was living across the country, my sister, who lives in Boston, and I immediately hired a whole team of people to help her. She wasn't quite ready to accept the fact that she was in mental decline, so within two weeks she fired everybody. We hired another team and told them they couldn't be fired. Over the next few years as the disease progressed, living in New York was no longer practical. The expense was exorbitant, and she was rarely leaving the apartment. My sister and I then made the decision to move her to LA to be near me and my family, where her grandchildren could visit her and I could directly oversee her care. I was researching residence homes nearby and found one that stood out as far superior to all the others, Silverado Beverly Place. Other residential care facilities had memory care "areas," but Silverado is completely and solely dedicated to memory care, and I had a strong feeling that this is where she should be.

I moved my mother into her new room and fixed it up with photos and things that were familiar to her and tried to make it feel as homey as possible. Initially, she was okay because it felt like she was on vacation in a fancy hotel. But as the months passed, she realized she wasn't leaving, and she started to withdraw and show signs of depression. At this point in a wheelchair, she couldn't leave physically, but she certainly checked out emotionally. Despite being in one of the best care facilities in the country for memory care, she was not doing well. Things really declined around the one-year mark. I'd show up and find her sitting away from the group, her head dropped to the side, surrendered to the desire to sleep. Often when people tried to talk to her, she looked blankly into the distance. She had lost interest in food, one of her great passions. My mother had always been the life of the party. I couldn't bear seeing her like this. I was heartbroken. *What have I done?* I thought. *Why did I uproot her from her home in Manhattan?* I was losing her much too quickly.

Then an idea came to me while I was at the dentist, of all places. Because it's LA, my dentist, who is a passionate and opinionated woman, also functions largely as a life coach. We often talk about personal matters. As I was telling her what was going on, I started to cry. "I just wish I could hire a comedian to make my mother laugh," I said, wiping my face with the paper bib.

"Why don't you?" she asked. "You should do that." I never honestly thought about doing it before the words passed my lips in that moment.

"Can I do that? How would I even find someone?" I wondered aloud.

"Well, just put it out into the world and see what happens."

And that's what I did. I went home and posted on Facebook, "Looking for a comedian, interested in gerontology, paid gig." My phone rang within five minutes. It was a friend from New York who had just seen my post on Facebook. (We're old enough that we still call each other.) She said, "Dani, you're not going to believe this. I was just talking to my friend, who now lives in LA, and she used to be a comedian and she doesn't want to do stand-up anymore. What she really wants to do is work with old people. She's talking to senior citizens on park benches for fun."

I called the woman up and we made a plan for her to meet my mother. I wasn't sure what to expect or if she could even get through to Mom. But I knew it couldn't hurt to try.

The day of that first meeting, we walked into my mother's room and I said, "Mom, this is my friend, she's from New York, too," as I steered her wheelchair so we could sit close together.

"What's up, Muriel?" the comic asked in that undeniable New York accent. My mother blinked. The comic moved in closer, putting her face at eye level with my mom. She turned away.

"You don't want to talk, do you, Muriel?"

Crickets from Mom.

"I get that," she said. "Some days I don't want to talk, either. When someone gets in my face, I think, 'Schmuck, do I look like I want to talk?'"

My mother turned her head back and smiled. Like any good comic, she repeated the punch line, this time with a little more moxie. "Schmuck, do I look like I want to talk?"

My mother smiled even bigger, then laughed and blurted out, "Schmuck!" like a kid getting away with saying a naughty word. She looked to us for a reaction. The comedian laughed heartily and then topped her. "Hey, schmuck! Do I look like I want to talk?" she asked again loudly, like a character from *The Sopranos*. "Schmuck!" my mother yelled back, laughing so hard she almost couldn't get the word out. I looked around, feeling slightly self-conscious about this boisterous schmuck-off. I was concerned not everyone would be able to appreciate the beauty of what was happening behind the *schmuck*s, but then I decided I didn't care because these two were having so much fun. It was the first time I'd seen my mother laugh heartily in a very long time.

A comedian! What a perfect fit for this job. Who better to be in the moment, to draw someone out, and, after years of dealing with hecklers, be undaunted by the volatility of a person in the grip of Alzheimer's, a brain disease with no known cure that affects some 5.7 million Americans? Needless to say, I hired this woman (she has requested anonymity). She started seeing my mother for eight hours a week, mostly around mealtimes or during an activity. Depression started to lift off my mother, and very quickly she began eating again and engaging with the community. She even started singing. It was wonderful to witness the transformation. I honestly wouldn't have believed it if I hadn't experienced it. The change was nothing short of dramatic. Almost immediately I thought, *This should be everywhere. Comedians need work and Alzheimer's/dementia patients need to laugh.* I mean, I thought it, but I didn't actually think that I'd be the person to make it happen. I was an actor, a teacher, an author, a mother, and sometimes I even paid attention to my husband. I had plenty to keep me busy.

But as fate would have it, soon after my mother's turnaround, another family in the residence home approached the comedian. "We see what you're doing and the impact you are having, and we'd like to hire you." She stepped outside and called me. "You mentioned that you wanted this to be in the world," she said. "Now we have another family asking for services, so I think you should do this."

I said yes to this family, and I saw amazing changes with this woman, too. I began to think more seriously about what it would look like to take our show on the road, so to speak. I decided to write an article about the experience for AARP to see how people would react to the idea. The article was so well received that my inbox was flooded with hundreds of responses from around the country asking for comedians for their loved ones. Clearly, I was on to something because there was a real demand for delivering laughter directly to those who needed it most.

Just after that, I got a call from my friend Monica, a comic actress I've known for years. Her mother had just been diagnosed with Alzheimer's and she had seen the AARP article. "Dani, I love this idea and I want you to come in and talk to my financial people, because I think it's something for our foundation to invest in. Write up some kind of business plan." *Write up a what?* I thought, but instead said, "Of course, I'd love to do that!"

I had no real idea how to write a business plan, but the phrase "Venn diagram" came to mind. I knew that the success of a real venture like this one boiled down to three components: Alzheimer's patients—easy to find; comedians—also easy to find; and money. I researched top markets where it made the most sense to get started, walked into the meeting in a silk shirt, pencil skirt, heels, and my diagram and walked out with a commitment from the room to finance the business for a year. Laughter On Call was born.

Around the time that we were launching Laughter On Call, I noticed the *Washington Post* running quite a few articles on innovative approaches to Alzheimer's. Someone there was clearly interested in the topic. I reached out to them through the PR team I had engaged that specifically works in the health care space and they went for it. Journalist Cathy Free wrote a really beautiful article about Laughter On Call, and we are so grateful for the exposure. From that, we received other interview requests and had stories published, and then we were invited on several television programs, CBS News, *Dr. Oz*, and *The Doctors*. The conversation I wanted, which was how to find ways to approach this very sad disease differently, and to mitigate the debilitating feelings of isolation and fear of people with the disease and their families, was started.

From there I started getting calls asking me to teach classes for entire staffs of care facilities and to run family workshops sharing simple tools that comedians rely on to create laughter and connection. Because I had taught at UCLA for so long and had identified these tools in *Take My Spouse, Please*, I already had the components of an educational program. So I leapt through that open door.

Although we've only been in operation for a little over a year, we are impacting the approach to the care for Alzheimer's and dementia patients around the US. We're even building communities in London and Toronto. The response has been nothing short of amazing. The testimonials have been pouring in, and each time I get a text or email

from a person who engaged us, I get choked up. To be clear, before we
ever send a comedian out, we send a five-page intake form to the families for specific information about their loved one. It's not just about
showing up with a rubber chicken and a couple of knock-knock jokes.
We are working for cognitive engagement with the client, connecting
through funny stories and experiences from their past and throwing
in images, ideas, songs, films, bad vacations, pets they loved or didn't,
all in the interest of connecting with them and making them laugh.
For example, one client in a remote town in Maine has early-onset dementia. He is also on the spectrum. Even though he's older, he has the
cultural taste of a five-year-old. He loves *Star Wars* and comic books
and Jim Carrey. We searched and found a comedian in his area who
also loves *Star Wars* and comic books. His family sends us the most
beautiful cards and emails about how much fun he is having. To think,
it was just an idea. To see it realized, to give people some relief and
laughter, is a profound gift.

After our appearance on *The Doctors*, the show gifted our services
to another guest who said she'd give anything to see her grandmother
laugh again. We made that happen for her. Not only are we helping the
patients, but we are helping families, caretakers, and groups all around
the country. In general, the Alzheimer's community is looking for alter-
native therapies to ease the difficulty of the disease because the number of patients is climbing, and finding a cure has not been successful.
Mental decline is not a joyful experience, so if we can pepper this very
painful reality with moments that are not painful and not sad, it eases
the tension in the whole community. I have proven tools to help do
just that. People like this option because it's non-pharmacological and,
as all laughter does, it eases stress, releases serotonin, exercises facial
muscles, and even burns calories! Side effects: less anxiety, less fear,
more connection, more joy.

{ Q & A }

What was your greatest opposition in this process?

Well, none of this was anything I planned on doing, so I didn't really know what to expect when we first started. But what happens rather frequently is that someone calls us and wants to hire us for a family member, but others in the family are resistant to the idea. They can't quite pair laughter with such a difficult experience. Most times, they are grieving over their loved one and what is happening, and that's completely understandable. My hope is that people will see that just because they themselves aren't ready to laugh, doesn't mean the Alzheimer's or dementia patient isn't ready to laugh. In fact, they need to. The number one—and two actually—feelings that people with the disease contend with are isolation and fear. Creating shared laughter addresses both of these instantly. You immediately feel less alone when you are laughing, and with our comics you feel comforted, so anxiety is also lessened. You can see this with your own eyes, but science is also touting the benefits of laughter—from releasing tension, reducing behavioral problems, stimulating oxygen delivery and blood flow, stimulating endorphin release, and strengthening the immune system. So we really need to make sure it's part of a holistic therapy approach for those who are daily riddled with fear and anxiety because they can't make rational connections with the outside world on their own anymore. Every sixty-five seconds, someone in the United States is diagnosed with Alzheimer's disease. We all need to be prepared with openness and armed with knowledge about this disease, because if it hasn't already, it's likely to touch your world in some way.

What are some of the ways your perception has changed from your younger years to now? How has it affected your approach to your work?

I finally got to a point in my life where I realized I really like helping people. I don't know that I would have said that twenty-five years ago. I was acting at the time, and I love acting. But I knew that all I had to offer wasn't being tapped as an actor. I knew there were ways to extend myself, I just didn't know what it looked like yet. I knew that sitting in a trailer waiting to be called to the set, although always grateful for the work, felt isolating. I've always been a performer who thrives on the feedback of a live audience, which is of course how I became a comic. I have come to appreciate that now, at the end of the day, I want to know I did something of value. I used to think that focusing on something new meant closing a door on my past, but I don't feel that way anymore. Discovering Laughter On Call and continuing to perform myself, both in clubs and for our clients, has taught me that we don't really know the end of the story until it's truly over. So you don't have to say good-bye to ways of expressing yourself, especially if you love it. You can simply say, what's next?

Did you have to break false beliefs about yourself and your abilities?

Well, I never dealt with money the way I do now. I mean, I've always made money and spent money and paid my bills, but that's very different from running a business. Right before my mother started losing it, she put me in charge of her estate, so that gave me some experience weighing options and making sound financial decisions. Turns out I'm good at it. Thank God.

What would you tell your younger self?

That it's going to be okay. And it might even be better than okay.

I was gripped with worry a lot of the time about what I was going to do to make a difference. I just couldn't see the path for me. I put a lot of pressure on myself, which made it difficult at times to settle down. I always felt like whatever I was doing it wasn't enough, whether I was sitting in a trailer on set, or nursing a baby, and don't get me wrong, I loved those things. I love acting, I love motherhood. I'm grateful for those things. But I wonder if I could have looked down the road to see what I'm doing today, if someone could have said to me, it's fine, whatever you're doing, because you're going to have this idea in your mid-fifties and it's going to incorporate all of these individual pieces of your life, so relax and take it all in—I maybe would have worried less. Not definitely, but maybe.

After my children started becoming more independent, and I published the second book on marriage, I embarked on a whirlwind fifteen-city tour to entertain big crowds of married people and even single people. As much as I believed in the message that people who laugh together, stay together, there were people like Esther Perel and John Gottman who were so far ahead of me on that front. That shared sense of humor was definitely part of their message, and I didn't feel I was going to have the impact I wanted to there. But the Alzheimer's community is ever growing and in so much need of innovative approaches. In my short time in and around that community, I haven't met someone better equipped with the skills and the personal experience to share the message that it's okay to laugh. In fact, it's essential for showing up and going the distance with Alzheimer's and dementia patients. I feel I have the opportunity to have an impact on people in this way. I can teach people how to show up for Alzheimer's and dementia with grace, generosity, and yes, laughter.

PATTY's POINTS

● **Be open to inspiration from unlikely sources.**

I'm a personal friend of Dani's, so her story is near and dear to my heart. I met Dani's mother a number of times early on in our friendship, before she developed Alzheimer's. I always knew her as a vibrant person, very engaged in the cutthroat world of New York City real estate. It's a shock to see the change in personality, or worse, the disappearance of it, that comes with an Alzheimer's diagnosis.

As with so many people in this book, Dani used her career experience—comedy—to tackle the issue of her mother's disease. I shook my head in amazement when I learned that it was her dentist who recommended that she take a step of faith. We never know where the inspiration is going to come from!

● **Look for creative ways to test the waters.**

As with many actors (including myself!), being good at business doesn't necessarily come naturally. Dani had to step out and learn how to create a business on her own. Fortunately, there are so many free resources online that can get you started.

Dani also wisely tested the waters through AARP to see if others in her position would be interested in her idea. Getting such a positive response was the encouragement Dani needed to push ahead. Now, not all second acts start with such immediate affirmation. If you have an idea in your head and heart, consider ways that you can test the waters and get some small-scale feedback from your target market before jumping in headfirst.

● **Your gifts are the foundation for your purpose.**

A common thread in many of these stories is the passion these second-act-ers have for the work they are doing. Because inspiration often comes from wanting to help a family member, people like Dani get deep satisfaction from seeing their life's work used in a whole different way—to serve not only their loved ones but many in the wider community.

Dani talked about always having a deep sense that there was something more for her to do. She often felt guilty for not pursuing something more meaningful, and her worry impacted her ability to fully enjoy her current season. Now it's clear that the time she spent developing her gift is the very thing that is the foundation for her purpose. If she hadn't taken the time to develop her gifts as an actor and comedian, she may not have the same insight, impact, and connections to do what she is doing today.

REFLECTION QUESTIONS

1. Where do you see yourself in this story? What part of Dani's personality, character traits, or journey can you relate to or identify with?

_____

_____

_____

2. What is your greatest takeaway from this story?

_____

_____

_____

3. Like Dani, have you worried about what you haven't been doing with your life? We've all been there. Make a list of anything you've worried about. Decide to let it go. Don't let heavy, unrealistic expectations keep you from moving forward.

_____

_____

_____

4. When was the last time you enjoyed a good belly laugh? Hopefully through this story you see the importance of laughter, not just for dementia patients but for all of us. Go find something that makes you laugh today!

_____

_____

_____

13

From Carpet Sales to the Red Carpet

The Second Act Story of Mike Monteleone

Mike Monteleone was in his fifties when he started his acting career by volunteering at the local community theater down the street. He was in carpet sales at the time and acting was just a hobby he enjoyed on the side. He poured his heart and soul into every production, even though he had no formal training. And then, as he approached his eighties, he found himself taking roles for TV commercials and popular shows such as *Grey's Anatomy*, *Parks and Recreation*, and my own show, *Carol's Second Act*. Mike is a prime example of what happens when you are willing to follow an opportunity no matter how small.

Here is Mike's second act story.

I was fifty years old when I first stepped onto a stage. I had no training. I had no experience. It was a labor of love. When someone would ask, "Do you love it more than your job?" I'd say, "Well, I wouldn't do my job for nothing, but I would do acting for nothing, so yes."

It all started when a little community theater opened up down the street from my home in Agoura Hills, California. At the time, I was working for a carpet manufacturer, managing corporate accounts. I had an interest in acting for a long time but never pursued it. Now an opportunity was practically in my backyard, so I decided, why not give it a try?

The building that housed the theater was originally an old 1930s grocery store with a gas station out front. The street it was on was the main road going from the San Fernando Valley to San Francisco, so this was a hub for travelers to get gas, or a drink, or whatever they might need for their road trip. It was a charming, nostalgic building with photos from the original store hanging inside. The theater was called the Stage Door.

The theater was so new that I auditioned for the second show they ever produced. I didn't make it. But that was okay. About a year later, I got a call about a Christmas show they wanted me to audition for. I accepted that role and, as they say, the rest is history. I became more and more active in the theater and landed bigger and more prominent roles. I worked from home, so I had a lot of flexibility in my schedule, but most of my off time was spent at the theater. Soon, I started volunteering on the production side and helped constructing the sets. And then, about ten years later, in 1991, I married the lady who opened the theater, and we've been together now for almost thirty years. So, acting changed my life in more ways than one!

The theater was like a family. There were only two of us running it. We didn't have a board of directors or shareholders to answer to, so we basically did what we wanted when we wanted. Veterans always got in free. When someone had a financial need, we would just do a fundraiser. My wife and I would get in fights about it because I would tell her, "Let's give the money after our expenses." And she would say, "No, let's give all of the money now." We once did a fundraiser for a lady with cancer, and we frequently did fundraisers for the local animal shelter. We were well-loved and supported by the community.

It was a small, intimate theater. There were only eight rows with forty-nine seats total, so you didn't have to project like you would in a larger space. It was more like acting in front of a TV camera. This was great because it prepared me for the next steps in my career. I never took any lessons or classes; I just grew with the experience I had onstage.

The time came when I wanted to start pursuing acting more seriously and look for paying roles. I had formally retired from sales in 1996 at age sixty-two, but I knew I wasn't ready to slow down with my acting. I had a friend who was doing extra work on-screen, small background roles in film and television. I took a few extra roles and was able to get my SAG card, but because of my commitment to the theater, I really couldn't add another thing to my plate. And the last thing you want to do in this business is audition for a role that you have to turn down due to unavailability. So I started to step back from my extra work to let some breathing room into my schedule.

Then something happened that none of us expected. In 2008, our landlord passed away and someone else bought the building. The new owner didn't want the theater there anymore, so we had to close it down. We were all heartbroken, and when word of our closing got out into the community, they responded with a petition. More than five hundred names were on it. It was hand-delivered to the new owner, asking her not to close down the theater. It was a lovely, heartfelt gesture. We were moved, but the new owner wasn't moved at all. We still had to go, so that was that. We've been closed now for eleven years, and to this day, we still get stopped on the street by people who tell us how much they miss the theater, and still it touches our hearts.

After the theater closed, I got an agent and started landing paid roles in commercials and on television. I just kept taking things one day at a time, one audition at a time. It seemed every year I would land two or three shows and then a commercial. Right now, I audition as often as I can and I enjoy it immensely. I'm grateful. I'm happy. I'm married to the love of my life. I'm eighty-five years old, so any work I get is a bonus. I never planned this life, but to me, it's better than I could have ever planned.

{ Q & A }

You said you had an interest in acting previously but never did anything with it. When did that interest begin, and why do you think the timing was right for you to pursue it at age fifty?

I grew up in Detroit. Back then I had no interest in acting. When I came to California in 1960, there was this appeal and glamour about the industry. I just became curious because it was all around me. So the interest was there, but it was subtle. I don't think I would have pursued acting if the theater hadn't opened up so close to me. However, the opportunity was there, so I took it.

What preconceived ideas did you have as a younger person about retirement or growing older?

None at all. I had no ideas. I was living in Detroit when some relatives came to visit from California. They talked about the warm climate and how it became routine for them to barbecue on Christmas Day. I got to thinking about the weather in Detroit compared to what they described in California. California sounded pretty good. So that's what made me decide to move back in the '60s. The sunny weather just sounded good to me, so I did it. The vision of grilling out on Christmas Day was the extent of my future planning! I really wasn't ever much on long-term planning because I figured I didn't know what my wants or needs would be in the future. I'm more of a live-in-the-moment kind of person, but it seems to have worked out for me.

What was it like learning your craft as an actor? How did you gain confidence in your ability? Were you ever nervous onstage?

Well, when I first started, I was always nervous going onstage. I froze up several times. It's safe to say I had no idea how bad I was . . . which was probably a good thing. I had the good fortune of having a little theater at my disposal. Because they needed actors, they tolerated some things that larger, more established theaters wouldn't. I was one of a few people in my age range auditioning so I was getting roles that probably would have gone to someone else if there were anyone else! I had my experience as a salesman, so I was comfortable presenting myself to people.

I would guess that in my first four or five roles, I froze onstage and completely forgot my lines. Eventually it got better. I realized it was my own fault, though. It wasn't that I didn't know the show or lines, but I let my mind wander, and when I lost focus, I froze up. But I stopped doing that. I appreciate the other actors who bailed me out during those times.

I also made the error of thinking that if I just said all of my lines exactly as they were written, and did what the director told me to do, then I was doing my part. I had a somewhat robotic performance style at first, and the director kept saying, "Have fun! Have fun!" I wasn't really sure what he was talking about. But eventually I learned how to really get into the character and become the character. Each show ran for eight weeks, so that was a lot of time to grow into a role. I just got better and more confident as I learned from the cast and director.

How long did it take before you felt ready to take a major role onstage?

I had the attitude that most unexperienced actors have—I felt like I could do any role. I did four or five small roles and then fell into a large role. I was doing a show where I had a small role and the director was also playing the lead. He asked me to come to the rehearsals and help him take notes as a director while he was onstage. About halfway through the show, he landed a large acting part on television and needed to quit, and I was the only one who could step in. I took that leading role. It was opposite the woman who is now my wife.

We did some powerful and emotional projects together. It took about three or four years before I really felt like I was coming into my own and honing my craft as an actor. I remember finally starting to get compliments on my performances, because in the early days, I didn't get any at all. Eventually, I was so immersed in my role that I stopped having an issue remembering my lines. I was able to ad-lib in character and no one ever knew, so that was fun.

What would you tell someone who is struggling to find the "next thing" for their life?

Many years ago, I was watching the Johnny Carson show. George Burns was the guest that night and they asked him that same question. He said, "Find out what moves you to passion, and do it." That made so much sense to me, and in the back of my mind that's always been a guiding principle for my life.

Sometimes you just have to try some things before you really find where your passion is. I would have never guessed I would have loved acting as much as I do until I tried it. So try some things, find your passion, and go after it. And that's the best advice I could give anyone. Find out what you love to do, and you will never work a day in your life.

PATTY's POINTS

- **It's never too late.**

Mike's story is a lot of fun, and a great example of a second act that doesn't have to be world-changing—it just changes your world. I met Mike on the set of my show *Carol's Second Act*. Now, if you're like me—a person who has lost both their parents—you immediately warm to elderly folks. That's how I felt about Mike. He had exactly one line, which consisted of one word: "Carol!" And he cracked us up every time he did it in rehearsal.

On the night of the taping, he was sitting quietly backstage by himself. I had a few minutes, and I wanted to chat with him, both because I like to make every actor feel welcome, no matter how small the part, and because I was curious about his career. It was such a surprise that he used to work in industrial carpeting, and that he only just started acting in his fifties! I was charmed by him and his story, and immediately thought others would be, too. That's why I wanted to include him in this book.

- **Follow your interests.**

Mike's second act wasn't born of tragedy or dire circumstances. He just took an interest in something and followed it. Mike seemed to take life as it came, without making any plans or having big thoughts and dreams about the future. What a surprise it must have been to him to get this completely new career so late in life!

● **Try new things.**

You see, a second act doesn't have to be about starting a company or a charity—it can be as simple as Mike's story—trying something new, staying curious, being open to learning. Mike got bitten by the Hollywood bug because it was in his community. If you look around in your community, what will you find? Even if, as in Mike's case, you don't think you can do something well, perhaps observe what's going on around you, make yourself available wherever needed, give something a chance . . . who knows what might be in store for you?

REFLECTION QUESTIONS

1. Where do you see yourself in this story? What part of Mike's personality, character traits, or journey can you relate to or identify with?

   _____

   _____

   _____

2. What is your greatest takeaway from this story?

   _____

   _____

   _____

3. Is there an interest that you've put on the back burner or something you are curious about that you'd like to explore? Make a list of at least three things that you are interested in.

   _____

   _____

   _____

4. Have you found yourself thinking that it's too late to pursue a
    dream? Don't let that limiting belief hold you back. Write down a
    statement of actionable intent toward a dream or goal. It might be
    small, but still. Start with, "I can and I will . . ."

    _____

    _____

    _____

14

Writing the Story She Didn't Choose to Live

The Second Act Story of Miriam Feldman

Miriam Feldman was a successful artist living in LA. Her husband owned the gallery where she held her first art show, and they were happily married with four beautiful, creative children. From the outside, Miriam's life was picture perfect, but her world was harshly turned upside down when their eldest son received a harrowing mental illness diagnosis. For the next decade, it was all she could do to navigate the nightmare and try to hold her family together. When the dust settled, Miriam began her journey of inner healing. She knew she needed to write a book to share her story and advocate for families who found themselves on a similar unchosen path.

Here is Miriam's second act story.

I was born and raised in LA, and ever since I could hold something in my hand, I always chose a paintbrush. I have a picture of myself when

I was maybe three years old standing in front of a huge chalkboard—I could barely talk and yet I was drawing an expansive mural of princesses and castles and knights on horses. My mother was an artist, and my father was a furniture designer, so they always supported my love for art, which fueled a great confidence in me and my ability. Before I ever went to college, I was making money as an artist. I started out doing custom Ketubah, which are ornate Jewish American marriage certificates. When I was in college, I got into painting house portraits, and after college I got into the movie business. Back then, they didn't have CGI, and so all the special effects were done by a team of creatives sitting around a table covered with paint, glue, and craft supplies. I was always the only girl, but it was so much fun. It was like hanging out in the garage with all the cool, weird, artsy guys who loved building, experimenting, and blowing things up. After I got married—to an artist—and we started having kids, I couldn't do the grueling hours anymore, but I wasn't about to give up art. This was back in the '80s and early '90s when faux finishing and sponge walls were all the rage. I saw an opportunity and started a decorative finishing business and worked with designers to paint businesses and homes all over LA. I would also take commission projects on the side. For example, I did a project for Disney where I concepted and re-created famous paintings with a Disney twist. For one, I re-created Monet's *Water Lilies* and added Mickey Mouse standing on the shore and his reflection in the water.

My work was always new and exciting and, because I love art so much, I had the best career in the world. I also did my own original paintings and would have shows and sell my work in galleries. My husband, Craig, and I lived in downtown LA in the late '70s, which is when the first real art scene hit the city. We lived in a warehouse loft and Craig owned an art gallery. We were completely absorbed in a world of art, and I loved every minute of it.

We had four kids between us. Our eldest daughter is Craig's from a previous relationship, but we married when she was very young, so I'm the only mother she's ever known. Our firstborn together was Nick, our son, and then we had two more daughters. When Nick was young, he was just the perfect boy—handsome, charming, and talented. He was a prodigy as far as art goes, and while it may sound so, I'm not being biased. I have four kids and I don't think all of them are art prodigies, but Nick definitely was. (I might be biased about him being perfect.) He made straight A's and was on track to becoming a world-class artist, set up for a spectacular life. When he was a teenager, he started having issues and odd behaviors, but don't all teenagers? Seriously, if you make a list of all the red flags for mental illness and you make a list of normal teenage behavior, they're basically the same thing. So we didn't think much of it; we just thought we had a difficult teenage son. But then the years went by, and his other friends at school started growing out of their issues, but Nick's issues seemed to get bigger. He developed extreme anxiety manifesting as nail-biting, sleeplessness, and secretiveness. He complained about weird thoughts he was having, which we later learned were voices in his head. His artwork became very dark with weird-looking people and disconcerting words. I was torn between an artist's respect for the quality of the work and a mother's apprehension about what it depicted. When he was in his late teens and finishing up high school, we knew there was something going on with him, but it wasn't until he was almost twenty that we got the diagnosis of schizophrenia.

Dealing with serious mental illness is like a gale-force hurricane that blows through your life, leaving total devastation. Anything not nailed down gets blown away.

By this time, our eldest daughter had moved out, but Nick was still at home, and our younger girls were eleven and thirteen. So here I was in the middle of my motherhood years and it felt like my life was being blown into a million pieces. At times I would slip into denial to cope. I was living a nightmare and I couldn't run; I couldn't wake up.

The way I deal with difficult things is by getting madly functional. So in the beginning I had this attitude that I was going to fix everything. I was figuring out a way to stabilize our son, shield the girls, hold my marriage together, and run a business with eight employees. I would put on my superhero cape by day and fall apart in the bathtub with a glass of wine at night. Or three. Who's counting?

The stigma, guilt, and shame of it all was completely overwhelming, and my husband was dealing with it by emotionally retreating. I felt so alone and didn't want to tell people what was going on. People can handle it when you say, "My son has depression." They can handle it when you say, "My son has diabetes." But when you say, "My son has schizophrenia," there's a completely different response. I tried to keep everything private, but word got out. We became known as the messed-up family of the neighborhood, as if it wasn't hard enough to be dealing with this horrific diagnosis.

As we sought treatment options, we learned that Nick actually had schizoaffective disorder, which is a combination of bipolar disorder and schizophrenia—the worst of all worlds. So he would have emotional ups and downs from being bipolar, and then he was just out of touch with reality because of the schizophrenia. Nick was on a mental roller coaster, and we lived on that roller coaster, trying different doctors and medications and therapies, anything to find a way to get him balanced out. Just when we thought a medication was working, it would stop working. Or he'd be good for six months, and then his brain chemistry would change and we'd have to start all over. It was a constant moving target.

About five or six years later, when one of our daughters was in college and the other was getting ready to go to college, Nick was finally stable and on the right medication. Of course, I still had to make him take it every day and look in his mouth afterward and make sure he swallowed it. I had been doing this for years because he couldn't be trusted to take it on his own. But finally being in a place of stability was so surreal. We made it. It was like that first ray of sunshine after the hurricane is gone, and you are grateful, but you still have a complete disaster all around you—you still lost everything. The worst was over, but I just felt numb inside. I didn't have a vision for the future. My greatest aspiration was to just love my family and do damage control until I died.

It's probably worth noting at this point that during this period, which I refer to as "the really bad ten years," not only did we receive Nick's diagnosis, but I was diagnosed with a brain tumor and had major brain surgery and major spinal surgery, my husband had a heart attack, and two of our daughters were diagnosed with cancer. So there was all that to deal with, too.

Through it all, I never stopped my art. It was like breathing for me, and I needed to breathe to stay alive. I was in some crazy sort of crisis mode for years, but I did my best to keep our lives afloat, even though I made a lot of mistakes in the process and my family was dealing with the fallout.

I don't know exactly when it happened, but sometime later, a fire was lit inside me to get back to taking care of myself. Before the bad ten years, I would go regularly to Pilates, but through all of this craziness I let it go.

There wasn't a Pilates studio in the area, but there was a yoga studio nearby, so I decided to check it out. Now I was edging up on fifty and pretty badly beaten up by life. I was worn-out and tired, and when I got to class I encountered a room full of bouncy twenty- and thirty-somethings talking about resilience, acceptance, and surrender. I just looked at them and thought to myself, *What do these unmarked women know about resilience? They don't have a clue.* But I went along with the class because I knew I needed something for me. As I listened, I realized there was a lot of truth in what was being said, and over the course of time, I discovered something about myself. I realized that so much inside me had been destroyed in terms of my preconceived notions about life and what I thought my family was going to look like, and my expectations of my children and how that reflected on me. All of it was shot to hell, and it was a hard thing to come to terms with. But with all of that gone, I was left with a lot of open space inside of me. I had room to explore other ideas that I would have previously dismissed—like doing anything else with my life besides art.

I had gotten help along the way from different organizations such as the National Alliance on Mental Illness (NAMI), and I decided that I needed to get involved with helping other people. I had already become sort of the "AA sponsor" for people dealing with mental illness because everyone I knew would give out my name and number to anyone they knew going through this. I would befriend people over the phone and share my story and what I learned. I had been considering writing a book for several years, and one day my husband finally said to me, "Well, if you are going to write a book, why don't you stop talking about it and go ahead and write it!" So that's what I decided to do. Every day I would go in my writing room and shut the door and write for eight or nine hours a day. It became my full-time job. I wondered if I could remember all the details, but as I started to write, it just all came out. I would be going about my day and a memory would come, and I would write it on a Post-it note and stick it to the wall and then try to organize it all in my writing room. Ironically, at one point, my desk looked like the workshop in the movie *A Beautiful Mind*. After about a year, I had a book. Or so I thought. It turned out to be a lot more work, but I was proud of myself for getting to this point.

With what I considered to be a manuscript in hand, I began researching the process to get my book published. I'm fairly old-school, so I didn't want to self-publish. I got on the computer and researched what to do next, and I learned that the next step is to get a book agent. Once you have a book agent, they become the bridge to a publisher. So I read all of these tutorials and did all of this research and it was recommended to find fifteen or twenty book agents that look like a good fit for your type of book and then you mail them a query letter, which is a request to have them represent you. After that, you hope for the best and wait for a response. Then if you don't get an agent, you send out another ten or twenty letters based on your responses. Well, when I started looking up agents and reading their requirements, I would see things like "If you don't hear back from us in twelve to twenty-four weeks, that means we are not a fit." I thought, *I'm sixty years old and I have lifespan issues here. I can't wait twelve to twenty-four weeks for an answer*. With time not on my side, I thought it might be better to stack the odds. I made it my full-time job for the entire month of January to send out query letters for eight hours a day. By the end of the month, I had sent out 976 letters. I continued into mid-February and, lo and behold, I got a bite. The online tutorials recommended that once you get a viable offer, you go back to the other agents you submitted to and let them know and give them one last chance to respond. So I went back to the other nine hundred and something agents and sent them emails letting them know I had an offer. By the end of this whole flurry, I had five viable offers from agents. It was incredible! Since then I've learned that people can spend ten years trying to get an agent, so it was a small miracle that I got one. And then the work began. It was a whole year of rewrites and editing with the agent and then I thought I had a book. My agent sent it out, and I got four good offers from publishers. I didn't want to automatically go with the biggest publisher. I went with the publisher who I felt most respected the book and respected me and my story, which was an up-and-coming publisher in Nashville, Tennessee.

With my book being published, I started looking for opportunities to volunteer more in the mental health community. I became active in NAMI and I got involved with Bring Change to Mind, the organization Glenn Close founded for education and advocacy around mental illness. They focus a lot on college and high school, and I'm on their advisory council and write a monthly blog. I also do public speaking and advocacy whenever I can. It's a whole new life for me, and I feel like I am just getting started. I went to the doctor recently for a checkup and I said, "You have to keep me alive for at least twenty-five more years because I have a lot to do!" I feel wonderful and I'm motivated—like I'm on fire. I've been painting my entire life, but I've never felt so artistically alive in terms of passion and care for people in the world.

Obviously, in a million years I would've never chosen to have this come about at the cost of my son. Schizophrenia is awful, and I would give the skin off my body for him to not have it. But because this happened, I am so much better of a human being, I am a much better person, and I listen and care more deeply, and it's all changed me for the better. My life is a story I would have never chosen, but I'm honored to have written it and to share it with the world in a way that can bring hope to other families on this same journey.

{ Q & A }

Miriam, you have experienced so much. We often hear that in these types of transitions, there is a grieving process and a letting go of the past. Did you go through that and what did it look like for you?

Well, yes, I went through grieving, but no, it has not been put to rest. All the other stuff—the tumors, cancer, and heart attacks—are all done and over, and I've moved past that season in general, but my son's illness brings a grief that I will carry with me always. I can't fix it, and I don't have the answers, but I'm living with it and I have a good life and that's the message I want to pass on—not that you can ever "get over it."

I'm very involved in the online community, and I hear all the time that for mothers dealing with this, it seems that death would be more merciful. That sounds weird to say, but as a mother, you are sitting there looking at your child the way you've always known them. They look the same, they sound the same. They are not broken or bleeding. They are right there in front of you and yet they are not. They are not themselves anymore. So it feels like a cruel joke. It's like life is saying, "You can have the outline of your child, but you can't have your child." And at the same time, you can't say good-bye because they are still in there. So you really don't have closure, because it's always staring you in the face. It's not an easy thing to live with, but you can live with it. You have to accept that it's not going away and it's not getting better. It just is.

But the good news is that I don't waste time anymore worrying about anything that isn't important. I'm not sitting around saying, "Oh, poor me, I had a brain tumor." Who cares? It's over. I don't sweat the little stuff anymore. And really, most of it is all little stuff.

Why do you think your family was able to stick together through all of this?

Well, at the risk of sounding like a Hallmark card, we love big. We aren't perfect and we get mad and we disagree, and we say things we shouldn't, but we are fiercely loyal and committed to each other no matter what. Now that we are on the other side of so much difficulty, I'm so proud of my family, because we're all still together and we take care of each other. Many families fall apart when tragedy strikes, so it's a huge accomplishment that we didn't. We may be a bunch of misfits, but we are a strong family. I'm fortunate that I don't have to wonder who will take care of Nick when I'm gone; I know his younger sisters will.

You said that you really feel "on fire" and like life is just beginning for you. What do you see ahead of you now?

There are still a lot of unknowns, but my plan is to impact as many people as I can with my story. I want to do more public speaking and more writing and get involved with as much advocacy as I can in terms of changing the law and changing the system. It's really unfortunate that care facilities and housing options for people are so expensive that most people could never afford it. I'd look at a place and think, Wow! This is gorgeous! Nick will have a great life here. *And then when I would talk to the administrator, I'd learn that the cost was upwards of $30,000 a month. There are good people tackling these types of issues, but what I think that I have to offer is my experience and compassion and understanding for other mothers going through this. Years ago, I felt so alone and isolated, and so I want mothers to understand they are not alone and there are resources to help. I also want to work to fight the stigma. To me, that's a big one. There should be no shame at all because it's something so far out of your control. So I'm telling my story and being open about it. It's scary and exciting at the same time. But I'm ready now more than ever to do this. My second act is about not acting anymore and being real and open and vulnerable with people. It's the best of me, and I'm ready to share it with whomever will listen.*

PATTY's POINTS

- **See your trials as a path to discovery.**

Miriam is one of those wonderful people you get to meet because you were all parents together in the neighborhood. I met Miriam through another mom who is an interior decorator. We were one of the lucky recipients of Miriam's master plaster work. Right alongside her was her wonderful and handsome son, Nick. Miriam is a tiny person with huge energy and paint splotches on her clothes—a true artist. She really knows how to put on a brave front, because until I read a draft of her book, I had no idea about all she had been going through. I was absolutely shocked to learn of the crises she was handling. Though I had heard Nick received a diagnosis of schizophrenia, I didn't hear too much else. Miriam is a strong person and never let on what was going on behind the scenes.

Now as an advocate for people with mental illnesses, Miriam is sharing her story, and I'm learning so much. She is truly an inspiration, not just because she has weathered so many storms, but because she really took hold of her vision and wrote her book. Many people tell you they want to write a book or play the piano or learn a new language (those last two are me). But very few people actually hunker down and put in the work it takes to accomplish those things. Miriam is one of the few. Maybe she was able to persevere, not only in writing a book but in also getting an agent and a publisher, because she had been through hell and back and was still standing at the end of it all. If we allow our trials and tribulations to be a means of discovering our own strengths, we can then move forward in confidence toward other goals.

● **Be willing to accept what you cannot change.**

It's important to note Miriam's attitude about Nick's illness: there is balance now, but it will never be the same, and Miriam has made peace with that. The Serenity Prayer comes to mind—we have to know what things we cannot change and learn to live with the "new normal" that a tragedy can bring.

Miriam made peace, but she didn't shy away from the fight in front of her. Her advocacy work is so necessary. Her story brings strength to others who are coping with the reality of mental illness in a child. Her transition from artist to author and advocate has transformed her life and the lives of those around her.

REFLECTION QUESTIONS

1. Where do you see yourself in this story? What part of Miriam's personality, character traits, or journey can you relate to or identify with?

_____

_____

_____

2. What is your greatest takeaway from this story?

_____

_____

_____

3. Miriam talks about feeling shame from the stigma associated with her son's diagnosis. Shame is a debilitating feeling that attacks our identity and makes us feel like there is something wrong with us. Guilt says, "I did something wrong." Shame says, "I am something wrong." When you consider your own life experiences, are you carrying shame because of something that happened to you? Oftentimes, the feeling of shame is the strongest over things that

are beyond our control. Today, make the decision to let go of shame and make room for what's waiting ahead for you.

_____

_____

_____

Giving Children a Voice

The Second Act Story of Rachel Arazashvili

Rachel Arazashvili was a nurse with a big heart and an infectious personality when one summer, she took a humanitarian trip overseas that changed her life. She was so moved on behalf of orphans in Africa that a deep drive and passion rose within her to begin advocating for orphans in the US. She pioneered several programs in her community, but little did she know that this would lead her to also advocate for children with disabilities—her newborn son included. The difficulties she encountered with her own son fueled her resolve to advocate on behalf of all children.

Here is Rachel's second act story.

As a single mom after a really difficult divorce, I worked my way through nursing school. I always had an interest in health and enjoyed caring for people, so it was a natural fit. I remarried in 2005, and shortly after, I planned to go on a trip to Africa to work in an orphanage and serve the community with an organization called the Christian

Women's Coalition. At the time, I had no idea how that trip would forever change my life.

In the months leading up to the trip, I was in the blissful stage of newlywed life with the man of my dreams. My life was finally everything I hoped for, and I wanted so badly to grow our family and have a child with him. However, I was in my forties by this time, so there were no guarantees. I had a son from a previous relationship, but my husband didn't have any children. Being Puerto Rican, my cultural upbringing places a great value on the ability to have children, so I was feeling ashamed that I couldn't get pregnant. I remember my grandmother saying to me in her broken English, "Rachel, you have a good man. You either need to fatten him up or give him a baby." I was also carrying guilt from having an abortion that I deeply regretted afterward. I wondered if that would affect my ability to get pregnant. I wondered if I was somehow being punished.

Right before I left on my trip to Africa, knowing how softhearted I am, my husband jokingly said to me, "Please don't bring back any children with you." In that moment, I didn't realize how difficult honoring his request would be. While in Kenya, one young boy in the orphanage stole my heart. His name was Peter. On my last day there, I picked him up to hug him good-bye and he said, "Me go home with you?" That was the only English he learned to speak and his words pierced my heart. I was so tempted, but I had promised my husband of three months that I wouldn't.

I left Kenya with such an intense feeling for orphans. It was all I could think about when I returned home. I began immediately sending financial support to Peter and love from afar, but I knew I had to do more. I had to do something for the orphans here in the US.

As I was researching ways to help orphans, I learned about the need for volunteer guardians ad litem (GAL). A GAL is a court-appointed advocate for children in the system—orphans and foster care. I threw myself wholeheartedly into this volunteer opportunity, knowing that it would keep me from stressing and obsessing about wanting to have a baby. I knew it would eat me alive if I didn't find a way to use up my emotional energy. Volunteer work provided a meaningful outlet.

After I completed my GAL training, I was thrown into the deep end when I took my first case. It was heart-wrenching. I wondered if I was in over my head. I represented three siblings whose mother was addicted to painkillers, and *her* mother was also addicted to painkillers. The three children were taken away and placed in the care of their grandmother on their father's side, since the father didn't want custody. From the outside, it's easy to say, "What's wrong with this woman, doesn't she love her kids more than pills?" Well, her three-year-old daughter had a rare and severe form of cancer, and she was not expected to live. While she was dealing with this crushing diagnosis, her eldest son, who was a teenager, was in a near-fatal car wreck where he was almost completely decapitated. The thought of losing two children was more than this mother could handle. She started taking medication for anxiety, which evolved into her addiction. She coped with her difficulty the way she had seen her mother cope.

The courts were recommending grief counseling for the middle child, a six-year-old boy, to prepare him for the death of his younger sister. This is where it was my responsibility to advocate on his behalf. How is a six-year-old supposed to process grief that he doesn't yet have, over losing a sibling that is still alive? I don't know that adults have the ability to do that. Besides, they weren't certain when or even if his sister would actually die. I advocated strongly to delay the grief counseling so he could enjoy happy days making good memories with his sister. The whole thing was a gigantic mess, but I would schedule regular visits with the mother and supervise when she had visitation with her kids. I encouraged her to stay on her addiction treatment program so she could one day have her kids back. I'm happy to report that a year and a half later, she was completely clean, remarried, and living a normal happy life with her family. Her daughter fully recovered from her cancer diagnosis. You would never know by looking at this family all that they had been through. I'm so grateful and honored to help bring restoration.

About six months later, I found out I was pregnant. Finally! My husband and I were elated, and I felt so beautiful in my first trimester. I had a man who loved me, I had a good job, my volunteer work was rewarding, and we were realizing our dream of growing our family. Things were just falling into place; however, being a GAL didn't seem like enough. I could only impact one family at a time. I had a drive inside to do more. I had two friends who also carried the same burden. We reached out to our church leaders about setting up an orphan outreach. They were completely on board and so in 2008 we launched All for Children Orphans Organization at Calvary Christian Center in Ormond Beach, Florida. We started by bringing in leaders from various orphan and foster care organizations in our county to talk to the congregation about volunteer opportunities and to also encourage adoption. We did clothing drives and set up an orphans' closet, to help meet the needs of kids in the system. We hosted adoption matching events. For example, one event was a huge carnival where the children could come play and meet potential forever families. I was pleased with the success of this endeavor, but in my heart I wanted to do more.

I was still volunteering as a GAL and had to go to the administration office for a group training one day. During one of the breaks, I started telling one of my colleagues about what I was doing with my church and sharing that I wanted to have a greater impact among the orphan and foster care population. Our conversation was interrupted by another GAL who overheard what we were talking about. She introduced herself and said, "My husband and I have a nonprofit organization called Kidds Are First, Inc. We raise money for the needs of abandoned, abused, and neglected children in the system. We are at a point in our lives where we can no longer give it time like we need to, and we are looking for someone to take it over."

I went home and discussed the opportunity with my husband, and we both agreed to take it over. I had no idea how to run a nonprofit, mind you, nor did I have any idea what it would evolve into. We ran the nonprofit out of our living room for the first year, organizing fundraisers and then supplying GALs with gift cards to purchase whatever items the children that they were representing needed. Over time, I realized that about 80 percent of requests were for clothing items. The needs were so great that at times I would receive requests and just pull things out of my own closet, items that I had stored since raising my first son.

One day I had an idea. Why couldn't we set up a storefront where kids could come pick out what they wanted? As it was, the adults were doing the choosing and kids just had to take what was given to them. I thought there had to be a better way to give these kids a choice, when most of their lives they've had none. In my early twenties, I lived in New York and managed several clothing stores, so I could see a storefront in my mind, but not in the budget. Because we were a donation-based nonprofit, we really didn't have the money to pay rent on a storefront, so I wasn't sure how that would work. Besides that, I was by then four months pregnant.

Right around that time, one day I was at home when I started having severe pain—the worst cramping I had ever felt. Something was very wrong. I fell to the floor in my room screaming, but my husband was working out of town and I was home alone. Thankfully, my phone was in reach and I was able to get ahold of a friend who broke through the front door to find me in agony in a heap on the floor. She took me to the hospital, where they ran some tests and told me, "Get comfortable. You aren't going anywhere until this baby is born." That was the beginning of a near-three-month fight for my life and the life of my unborn son.

I was diagnosed with placenta accreta, which is a fairly rare condition where the placenta attaches incorrectly. It's a very complicated condition with a high risk of fatal hemorrhaging. I was completely bedridden in the hospital. The only thing I could do was read or listen to music, so I would put classical music on my belly, Mozart and Bach. Every three days they did an ultrasound and bloodwork to track what was happening. I had five life-threatening bleeds while I was there, and on top of that, I contracted a staph infection and went septic, nearly dying a sixth time.

After two and a half months of total bedrest, I appeared more stable, and so they allowed me to get up to go to the bathroom only—which felt like walking a mile after all I had been through. On Sunday, April 19, 2009, I stood up to start the trek across the room when I felt a gush of warmth down my leg. I knew immediately it was another bleed, so I pressed my emergency button. The staff flew into my room and went right into action. During the previous four bleeds, they would immediately place internal clamps on me, which always felt like being stabbed with knives inside. This time, they took me straight to surgery. It was complete chaos, and I could sense that everyone was nervous about what was happening. They would need six different surgeons for a cesarean as complicated as mine, but it was a Sunday, so they had to do major emergency surgery with a skeleton crew. There wasn't time to call anyone in. I can remember them strapping my arms down on each side as the anesthesiologist put the mask on my face. It felt like he was smothering me. Everything was happening so fast I just said a prayer in my mind: *God, if it's my time, take me. But I know I have so much more work to do.*

And then I was out.

I woke up in recovery with my husband standing by my bed. It was a huge relief to see his face, but what about our baby? Before I could get a word out, he said, "It was a miracle. When they removed the placenta, there was no bleeding at all." The medical staff was completely shocked because they could see on the scan before surgery where the blood vessels were improperly imbedded, and they were expecting the worst. But when they removed the placenta, it was as if the blood vessels had been cauterized. No one could explain it.

Our son, Noah, was born at twenty-eight weeks, weighing 4 pounds, 8 ounces. He was in the NICU for three weeks while his lungs finished developing. When the day finally came to go home we were so relieved. I'm sure I had PTSD, but I didn't have time to worry about it. I had a newborn to care for, on top of the fact that I had to relearn how to walk and use my body. My muscles were completely atrophied, so any small task felt like a huge undertaking. My body was a complete disaster, but my heart was strong. Something happened inside of me during that three-month fight for my life. A strength grew inside me, a new confidence and resolve. I came to face-to-face with death and I walked away—with my child. I felt like I could do anything, and I knew I would fulfill the mandate in my heart as a mother and on be-half of orphans.

Noah wasn't an easy baby, so I had to push off my plans to try to open a storefront. Thankfully, I had a team of volunteers who worked with me. Because I wasn't getting much sleep, I had to delegate a lot of the responsibility of Kidds Are First for a while. Noah didn't like sleeping in his crib, only in his swing. He would eat and then vomit profusely. He would get constipated and then developed severe eczema. He wasn't happy at all compared to my first son, Christopher, who was in high school by this time. When Noah was around four to six months old, we finally started to see him sparkle. With my first son, I thought I had failed him by not teaching him the importance and joy of reading, so I decided to get ahead of it this time and started Noah on the Your Baby Can Read program. He was walking at seven months and reading flash cards around eight or nine months. I would show him one that read "Arms up" and he would put his arms in the air.

When he was almost twelve months, if felt like the right time for me to get back to my dream of opening the store. I had resigned from my nursing job when I went into the hospital, so I had some time on my hands. I felt like I was moving into a better place as a mother and I was equipped with fortitude and determination. However, I still didn't have any money. I wanted to at least get connected with the local business community and perhaps tap into some resources, so the first thing I did was become a chamber member in Ormond Beach. I attended my first meeting, which was held in the local MBA business center. A representative of the business center gave the keynote address and then proceeded to explain that the owner was holding a contest. The winner would receive free rent in his business center for a full year. I nearly came out of my chair! That is exactly what we needed for Kidds Are First. All I had to do was submit a business proposal to be considered. Of course, I'd never done that before and had no idea how to write one. But I sat down at my computer and I wrote from my heart. I shared my vision and plan for the clothing store for orphans. Then I said a prayer and hit Send. Several days later, I received a phone call. I won the contest.

The next day, the *Daytona Beach News-Journal* called to interview me and asked what our next steps were. Everything happened so fast, I didn't have any next steps. I had a bin full of clothes that I had been collecting in my living room, but that wasn't going to get a storefront started. So I reached out to a friend who worked with local homeless shelters and she had a surplus of items to pass on. Then she and I worked together to make calls and collect additional items. Somehow, we gathered enough items to get started, and I set up the store like I had set up those clothing stores in New York so long ago. Lo and behold, we had our grand opening of KR Fashions complete with ribbon cutting that was featured on TV News 13 and in other local news publications. The community embraced us wholeheartedly, and from the time we opened, we just kept growing. We have been honored with numerous awards and recognitions over the last decade, thanks to the amazing team of volunteers who work with me to make it all happen. There's no way I could have done it on my own.

Now, ten years later, we are in a building that is three times the size of where we started and we now partner with fifty local organizations to provide all basic essentials and 100 percent free clothing for our specific clientele of abandoned, abused, and neglected children. We work with group homes, schools, churches, foster care organizations, GALs, grandparent associations, and more. It starts with an email request to me, and I review the case. Then we set up an appointment for the children to meet one of my volunteers at the store for a private, personal shopping experience. When you enter the store, it looks like you are walking into a Gap, so the kids immediately feel special and we treat them like celebrities. Some of them have never even been shopping before or ever had a choice about what to wear. They've lived their entire lives in hand-me-downs. We encourage them, love them, show them how to dress and put outfits together. We have a prom room for teens; we have toys, makeup, suits for job interviews, and more. We teach young men who are aging out of the system how to tie their ties and give them basic interview etiquette so they feel prepared for a job interview. We have been so embraced by the community that we are overflowing with donations now. We have a completely full store and three storage units full of stuff! And people graciously give quality items, designer purses, duffel bags, suitcases, and backpacks, too. As we spend time with the kids in the store, the stories they share are heart-wrenching. Their resilience is amazing, and we pray that our interaction deposits hope into their hearts.

When I look back over the last decade, I'm overwhelmed with gratitude for so many things, and at the same time, I don't know how I made it through. You see, right around the time I opened the store, Noah started declining and having problems again. His sleeping was off, he couldn't do car rides. He would just scream constantly. The doctors told me it was just his temperament. He'd have eczema so badly we'd have to wrap his arms in gauze to keep him from scratching while he was at day care so I could work in the store. When he was two years old, he started doing peculiar things like lining up his toys, flapping his arms, and spinning. When I would pick him up from day care, I hated the questions and comments from the workers: "Can he hear okay?" "Can he pay attention?" "He just sits and watches the fan spinning." At that point, life just got really difficult. Family members would look at us and say, "Is he okay?" He would just scream so much around them. I didn't know what to do. No one did. All I knew was that this child I prayed for, this gift to me and my husband, was struggling.

One of my friends had enough courage to talk to me about having some specific testing done. When he was two and a half, the doctor described his condition as "highly probable autism." Highly probable autism? I didn't even know what that meant, but the nurse in me went to town and just started researching like crazy. There was no one locally who I could talk to about it. No one in my circle knew I was dealing with this and I didn't know anyone who had a child with this diagnosis. All I had was the internet. I felt completely overwhelmed and went into a depression, hibernating at home. Thankfully, I had volunteers managing the store and because we operated by appointment only, I had a lot of flexibility. I would stay up all hours of the night researching to see how I could help him. When I started learning about possible causes and triggers, I became angry. But I didn't know who I was angry at. I was angry at the world. I was angry at everyone in the world. I was angry at people who even asked me, "How are you?" Needless to say, this caused a huge strain on my marriage. It was an emotional struggle for both of us. My husband was in denial for the first year, and I felt like I was the only one trying. I just felt completely alone.

My research finally led me to a professional who had some direction for me that worked. We started with Noah's diet. When I took gluten and casein out of his diet, Noah finally started responding to his name. This was a child who would bang his head on the floor and injure himself. He would scream constantly and kick and have fits. I couldn't even go shopping. I would have to abandon my cart when a meltdown started, out of the blue. It was a struggle to even drive my older son to high school in the mornings because Noah would sit in the back and scream so intensely that I thought, *If I don't pull over, this kid is going to pass out, or choke*. He wouldn't make eye contact, and he practically never slept. His melatonin system wasn't working, so he would be up all night and then fall asleep finally at 5:00 a.m. I was the only one who could manage him, or tolerate him during this season, and I would often take him to KR Fashions with me and just put him in his playpen with his favorite toys while I worked.

Then one day, I had an experience with him that impacted me more deeply than my experience at the orphanage in Africa. We were in the kitchen and I had set him on the counter to tie his shoe. He was starting to meltdown. He was waving his arms wildly and accidently smacked me hard right in the face, sending my glasses flying across the room. It was a pivotal moment, and something rose up in me. I picked him up with "mamma bear" love and resolve and marched into the living room and sat him on my lap in the recliner. I put my hands on both sides of his cheeks and brought his face close to mine. I looked him right in the eyes and through my tears I said, "I know you are in there and I love you! I will do anything I can to get you out of there." He just stopped and looked at me. For the first time in a very long time, we had a connection. His eyes met mine and then he hugged and kissed me.

And that's why I never give up. Autism doesn't have my son. He is in there. There is hope for my son and hope for all children. That's why I do everything I can to give back to children who are alone and suffering because I know what it's like to have a child struggling just to exist in this world. I deal with children every day who are abandoned, abused, and neglected. Many of them are on the autism spectrum as well, placed in the system because their parents can't deal with them and can't afford to get help. These children are largely overlooked and unseen by society, and my purpose is to do everything I can to give these children a voice.

{ Q & A }

Wow. What an incredible journey you've been on. Your volunteer work is so emotionally involved and all-consuming. How do you find balance, and what do you do to invest in yourself emotionally?

Well, I'm not always good at that part, I'll be honest. But after running the store for a few years, and managing the stress of all the heartbreaking stories, and raising a child with autism, and homeschooling him, and even fostering some myself, I was getting burned out and I knew I needed to do something to invest in me. I decided to look for a hobby to give myself a mental break, but I wasn't sure what to do. Noah was nine years old at the time, an accomplished pianist and musician, and had just released his first CD on iTunes, Rhythm Unspoken. *A magazine called MyHealth wrote a story about us and the headline read "Mom Helps Child Find His Voice." It was a beautiful article, and we received a lot of attention from it. One day, I got a phone call from the director of the Ms./Mrs. Corporate America Competition. She told me that she had read the article. She said, "You have an amazing platform. I want to invite you to compete in our 2018 pageant competition." I almost busted out laughing. Seriously? Me? A beauty pageant? At my age? I thanked her for the call and told her I'd think about it, but I didn't mean it. I thought it was somewhat silly, although I appreciated the organization's focus on supporting innovation and women in business. My husband and my parents convinced me to compete, so I spent the next year preparing for the pageant. I started taking ballet to help me walk better in heels, I got back into the gym, started yoga, and forced myself to sleep and eat right. I thought,* If I could connect with one person on my platform, orphans and autism, then it would all be worth it. *Looking back, this opportunity gave me an "excuse" to pamper myself more than I had in years. It was exactly what I needed to refresh myself. I wasn't expecting to win. In fact, I didn't want to win. I had enough on my plate and I certainly didn't need anything else to do.*

Well, all of my preparations paid off in more ways than I bargained for. I took home all the first-place awards in every category I entered and ultimately won the pageant. Surprise!

I had a lot of preconceived ideas about beauty pageants, but after serving for a year, I have a whole new respect for the industry. I did over seventy events in fourteen months, which apparently was more than anyone before me, and I was presented with the President's Volunteer Service Award signed and sealed by the White House. When I was doing my final walk and preparing to crown the 2019 winner, the emcee asked what I was going to do next. I said one word, "Rest," and the crowd erupted with laughter. But I'm grateful for the opportunity because it opened a lot of doors for my nonprofit.

What kind of doors were opened through the experience of being Ms. Corporate America?

Well, first of all, it helped me grow a lot as a person. You have to be extremely confident to walk anywhere with a crown on your head. It took me some time to get past feeling like a little girl playing dress-up, but the crown is a marketing piece for both the organization and the cause of the winner. The crown made people stop to talk to me. I was able to get meetings and create new partnerships. For example, there is one high-profile organization in our community that does a huge benefit every year to collect toys that they distribute to organizations who help children. I tried for three years in a row to get on their donation list with no success. But when I walked in the door with a crown on my head, it got everyone's attention. The founder came out and spoke to me himself. Now everyone on the board knows me and they support us every year. Sure, as a pageant queen, I learned a lot about hairpieces, contour, and body shapers, but I'm thankful it helped me to be more effective to help the children in need in our community.

It also opened the door for me to join the Florida Developmental Disabilities Council, so I am studying to be a policy maker. There's a team of us who will address policies for disabled individuals regarding education, medical, housing, employment, and more. I've spent years advocating for kids, one at a time, now I'll be advocating for the kids of the entire state . . . and who knows where that will lead.

What's it like going from working for a living to working for a purpose?

Everything I do is 100 percent volunteer. It's emotionally draining yet still so rewarding every time I see the kids who come into the store and hear their stories. I love having the opportunity to encourage them and build relationships when possible. Every year I think, Can I do this another year? *But even if I wanted to do something else or go back to school, who would take care of Noah? A lot of mothers with autistic children are limited with their choices.*

I never looked at Kidds Are First as if it belonged to me, but I see myself as a steward for this organization. It's been a challenging journey of servitude, nothing I ever dreamed I would be doing in my younger years. It's really molded my character and has expanded my love for people, especially my love for children. When I first started pursuing volunteerism, I wanted to get my degree in counseling, and I started in that direction but had to lay it down when I was pregnant. I realize now, when you have a passion for something, you don't have to have a degree behind your name to get it done. I also learned that sometimes you have to let go of the picture of what you thought life would be like in order to find joy in the story you are living. Working for a purpose is priceless!

What's next for you?

Well, policy making for the state is a huge next step for me personally. We will be tackling issues that have been largely ignored for years, particularly in the area of education and employment opportunities.

My state is fiftieth for addressing the needs of the special-needs com-munity, the very worst in the nation. There's funding for programs and policies in place, but people don't really know how to execute them. So I'm learning about all of this and what we need to do in order to solve some of these problems.

I homeschool my son because services are so woefully inadequate here in the public school system, and it's no secret. There are inves-tigations going on right now for discrimination and abuse of autistic children in the school district. My son wants to go to school, and I be-lieve the right school would benefit him, but there isn't an option right now. I've considered starting a school for special-needs kids. There are thousands of moms who are giving up their careers to take care of their autistic children because there isn't adequate care and education in the public system. So it's a huge problem, and I hope in my new role as policy maker that I can help make a difference.

What would you say to someone who is ready to do more, but maybe they don't know what they want to do next?

Start volunteering. Explore where your passion is and see what comes easily. Find a need and fill it. Start doing something with what you have in your hand. People ask me all the time about how to start a nonprofit, and I say go volunteer at one first. As a volunteer, you will learn from people who are running the organizations. Start with what you can do and then you will know what you need in order to take your next steps.

PATTY's POINTS

● **View life's interruptions as interruptions, not ending points.**

Gosh, it seems as if Rachel has multiple acts going on at the same time! She's definitely a person with a passion for life and for philanthropy, and someone who likes to take on a lot! I relate to this a bit. I think that because my career started so much later in life, I want to grab every moment and make the most of the time I have left. Rachel seems to have that same energy! Though I have never met Rachel in person, the power of Rachel's personality really comes through in her story. She has such drive! How else could she come through a difficult pregnancy and take over Kidds Are First? Rachel's second act is interesting in that the charity wasn't her idea originally, but when she took it over, she came up with a completely new way to increase its impact—by distributing the clothing in a store-like setting. It's good to note that she had the inspiration long before she could see it come to fruition. Her difficult pregnancy interrupted her vision for a time, and then even after she had available time, she had to take the interim step of joining the chamber of commerce to make connections. Rachel's route seems a bit circuitous on the surface, but each step she took had a pragmatic reason behind it.

Her beauty queen status is a wonderful and surprising aspect to her very full life. Though it seems unconnected to her work, winning pageants (and workin' that crown!) has served to make connections and raise funds where previously Rachel couldn't get through the door.

My takeaway from Rachel's story is that we shouldn't see

unexpected events in our life as interruptions to our goals or dreams, but as opportunities to reassess and regroup.

● **Optimism helps.**

Rachel's passion for all things is accompanied by a positive outlook, a belief that she can actually do something about the issues she cares about. Having this outlook has mental and physical benefits for a person. Psychologist Michael F. Scheier noted these effects in his ground-breaking research on the power of positive thinking:

> I think it's now safe to say that optimism is clearly associated with better psychological health, as seen through lower levels of depressed mood, anxiety, and general distress, when facing difficult life circumstances, including situations involving recovery from illness and disease . . .

Optimists are not simply being Pollyannas; they're problem solvers who try to improve the situation. And if it can't be altered, they're also more likely than pessimists to accept that reality and move on.

We can safely say that Rachel's positive outlook on difficult circumstances—both in her personal life and in the community around her—have definitely enabled her to create a number of new acts in her life. I can't wait to hear what she does next!

REFLECTION QUESTIONS

1. Where do you see yourself in this story? What part of Rachel's personality, character traits, or journey can you relate to or identify with?

   _____

   _____

   _____

2. What is your greatest takeaway from this story?

   _____

   _____

   _____

3. In the same way that Rachel so desperately wanted to have another child, is there a dream or desire that is causing you to be anxious while you wait? Have you considered outlets to redirect that emotional energy?

   _____

   _____

   _____

16

Golfing Fore a Purpose

The Second Act Story of Betsy King

Betsy King is a professional golfer whose name dominated women's golf for nearly two decades. She played on the LPGA tour for twenty-eight years with thirty-four career wins total. In 1995, Betsy was elected to the World Golf Hall of Fame and inducted into the LPGA Hall of Fame. She retired from the tour in 2005, but her life's work was just beginning. In 2007, she founded Golf Fore Africa, after going on a trip where she saw firsthand the plight of AIDS orphans throughout Africa. By enlisting the support of LPGA golfers, Betsy and Golf Fore Africa granted more than $9.4 million to build health clinics and bring clean water to villages in Zambia and Rwanda.

Here is Betsy's second act story.

I was born in Reading, Pennsylvania, and grew up focused on sports. I played golf collegiately at Furman University on the 1976 national championship team. I was low amateur at the 1976 US Women's Open, then joined the LPGA Tour in 1977. In the '80s, I joined a faith-based organization called the LGPA Christian Fellowship, which met on Tuesday nights of tour weeks for Bible study and organized various mission projects. I initially joined because I thought it might give me something else to focus on, to help me manage the ups and downs and the stress of my career. But over time, my convictions grew deep and my faith grew stronger. I felt compelled to give back in any way I could and use whatever influence I had to help others.

In 2001, our Tour Fellowship Group chapter held a fundraiser to help a village in Tanzania. We worked with an organization called World Vision, which is the largest Christian international non-governmental humanitarian organization in the world, working in nearly one hundred countries. This was my first connection to anything in Africa. After our fundraiser, I had planned a trip to go to Tanzania in person. However, when the terrorist attacks on 9/11 occurred that same year, my trip was canceled.

My last year on the LPGA tour was 2005, and leading up to my retirement, a friend gave me a book about finding meaning in the second half of life. The basic premise of the book was that we spend the first half of life focused on building security, and the second half we should spend focused on giving back. I had already been seriously considering how I would spend the next season of my life, so the message in the book really resonated with me. It caused me to really dig deep. It motivated me even more toward humanitarian efforts, specifically in Africa.

In 2006, I reached out to a man named Dana Buck, a connection I made at World Vision back when we held the fundraiser five years earlier. I told him that I had it in my heart to do something for Africa, but I wasn't sure what. Dana suggested that I go to Africa in person and told me that World Vision happened to be organizing a trip with a small group of women to observe the effects of poverty and HIV/AIDS on women and children in Rwanda, Kenya, Tanzania, and Zambia. This seemed to be the perfect opportunity for me. Little did I know how that trip would impact the course of my life.

When we arrived in Africa, our group met up with some other World Vision volunteer caregivers who were helping AIDS victims— doing things like giving them baths, taking them to get medicine, and helping their families get tested. The first home we visited belonged to a woman who lost her husband to AIDS. She had five kids and feared that three of them might be HIV-positive; however, she couldn't afford to have them tested. When we arrived, she was cooking one egg for her entire family. It was all she had. The World Vision team went right to work helping to meet her needs and the needs of her family.

The next year when I returned, she was a completely different woman. She had become a volunteer caregiver. By a sheer miracle, none of her children tested positive for HIV. She was so grateful for the help she received that she wanted to give back, and that's what it's all about—empowering people to take care of one another.

That first trip was the first time I was able to see the extent of the poverty in Africa, and how it affected women and children in particular. It was heart-wrenching. Everyone on the trip was so moved by what we experienced that we all returned home with a sense of responsibility. We were resolved to help find solutions.

Among the twelve of us on that trip was a friend of mine, Debbie Quesada, who was also from Scottsdale, Arizona, where I live. We had worked on some charitable projects in the past, so when we came back, we decided to partner up to think of new ways to help those women and children. Debbie and I began talking and planning. With my twenty-eight years as a member of the golf community, it was a natural next step to use golf as a vehicle for fundraising.

In general, the golf community is extremely generous. Each week at any LPGA event, there are Pro-Ams to help raise money for different causes. With a passion in our hearts for the people of Africa, in 2007 Debbie and I formed Golf Fore Africa, a 501(c)(3) nonprofit with this simple mission: *To bring hope and change to children and families living in extreme poverty in Africa by empowering the golf community to support transformational programs that enhance the families we serve.* Because we were already familiar with World Vision and their excellence, efficiency, and economies of scale, it made perfect sense to partner with them to execute our mission. Golf Fore Africa would raise the money, and World Vision would execute the programs.

We began setting up fundraising events right away such as

auctions, golf tournaments, one-day clinics, golf events, and luncheons. We've been overwhelmed by the response and success. We typically host events in Florida, Arizona, New York, California, and Texas, but our goal is to continue growing and expanding.

Over the years, we've launched a number of different projects. We've partnered with both World Vision and Habitat for Humanity to fund and build forty-five houses, each costing $13,000. They were simple homes, but a needed upgrade from the thatch-roofed huts and dirt floors the recipients were living in—many of them children. We also raised money to open a health clinic in Rwanda that now serves more than twenty thousand people. We worked on a school in Zambia, adding classrooms and sleeping quarters for staff, and also helped ship thousands of backpacks filled with necessities such as soap, blankets, washcloths, pens, pencils, and notebooks for the children.

For the last three and a half years, we have been centered on bringing clean water to rural villages. Clean water changes everything. It's hard to overstate how critically important this work is. There are 844 million people in the world who live without clean water. That's nearly one in ten people worldwide, twice the population of the United States. It's estimated that one thousand children die every day from waterborne diseases. Giving clean water means giving life.

When a village doesn't have its own water source, the women and girls of the village are responsible to go collect the water. They spend hours every day walking to the nearest source. Over the course of her lifetime, the average African woman will walk the distance of the earth to the moon just to get clean water. Spending hours every day fetching water prevents young girls from attending school and keeps women from tending to their families or pursuing jobs outside the home. When a community gets a clean water source, like a simple well with a hand pump, the lives of their women and girls begin to change radically. They get back hours and hours every day. Children can be children; they have time to play and go to school. Women can start businesses, improve their homes, grow crops, and take charge of their own futures. When women are empowered, families become empowered. When families are empowered, communities are empowered.

Golf Fore Africa is currently working on bringing clean, fresh drinking water to more than 200,000 people in rural Africa. We are committed to helping end the global water crisis by 2030. So far, we've installed 310 wells, impacting 130,000 people. Each well brings clean water to around 300 people, on average. Hand pumps allow water to be generated without electricity, and once the wells are drilled, World Vision works with the villagers to maintain them and ensures they are equipped for long-term sustainability. A recent UNC water institute study concluded that after twenty years, more than 80 percent of the wells that World Vision installed are still in operation, so that's a huge success rate.

We have also provided thirty-six mechanized water systems for health clinics and schools. A mechanized system uses solar power to pump water from an aquifer into a large storage tank. The water then travels through pipes to sinks and taps inside the facility, so they have running water and indoor toilets. One mechanized water system brings clean water to thousands of people.

I recently returned from my twenty-fifth trip to Africa. On one of my recent trips, I brought a couple of donors with me to dedicate four wells. In the US, we often take the conveniences we have for granted. We have clean water anytime we want. But imagine if you couldn't drink clean water without walking for hours to get it. That's been the reality for many people their entire lives. So when a well is installed, it's a joyous celebration for everyone in the community. There's dancing and singing, and water. Lots of water!

My work with Golf Fore Africa is some of the most rewarding work I've ever done, but I also have another way I'm giving back at this stage in my life. As much as I am able, I mentor young girls, junior golfers, collegiate golfers, and even golfers on the professional tour. I've been playing golf for close to fifty-five years now, so I feel like I have a lot to share with the next generation and it's something I really enjoy. Growing up as a female athlete, I didn't get this type of support from other women, so I think it's very important to connect with young women and invest in their dreams on and off the golf course. I am on the board of the Junior Golf Association of Arizona. I am involved with the local LPGA Girls Golf Club. I've also had the opportunity to speak at different collegiate women's events. Mentoring young women gives me a sense of satisfaction in a different way from the work I do with Golf Fore Africa. My hope is that I can share skills and strategies, but also that they will find that sense of purpose that I found, to use their abilities to give back.

I am only one person doing what I can, but if I can influence others to step out and do all they can, together we will have an exponential impact. So this is my focus now: empowering women and girls to empower others, whether it be on the golf course or in the remote villages of Africa.

{ Q & A }

Did you have any idea when you were younger that this is what you would be doing with your life?

I grew up in the church, so the idea of helping others and doing missions work overseas was a part of my upbringing. But my faith and conviction wasn't that deep—until I got on the tour. I found myself questioning my life's meaning as I strove to handle the stress and the pressure I was experiencing. I wondered, Is this all there is for me? *Once I got involved with our fellowship group and started doing some service projects in the community, things began to change. I had gotten involved in some Habitat for Humanity projects in different places around the country. I became a member of the board of the Fellowship of Christian Athletes. I went to a number of junior golf camps to serve. I traveled to Romania twice to visit orphanages. That's when my faith began to really deepen. I realized the importance of helping others and getting outside yourself. I would say that I've been involved with charity work from the time I was about twenty-five years old. The funny thing is that I remember praying, "Lord, am I supposed to stay here on the tour or do you want me to go to Africa and be a missionary?" I kept having success on the golf course, so I stayed there. But that seed was in my heart, and it wasn't until twenty-five years later, in 2006, that I ended up going to Africa, but not quite in the same way that I had imagined. So it's interesting how all of that worked out.*

What was it like to go from playing golf to running a nonprofit? Did you ever feel like you were in over your head or wonder what you were doing?

For me personally, it was having my friend Debbie Quesada partner with me. It was the two of us that started this and, early on, we happened to meet someone who was raising money for World Vision through a charity that hosted sport-related fundraisers. They had all the information on how to form a nonprofit, so we had a model to follow. Then we had another contact who directed us to an attorney, who helped us complete the paperwork required to file for nonprofit status.

I know I couldn't have done it by myself, so I have to give credit to Debbie. She runs the organization full-time now. When we started, the office was in my house, and it was just the two of us. She was part-time. Now we have four full-time employees, and we've already raised more than $3 million this year alone. So it just came together as we took one step at a time. I've been very blessed.

I continue to meet new people all the time and reconnect with people in the golf community who want to support what we are doing. I'm glad that I can help reach people that World Vision wouldn't normally.

Did you ever consider moving to Africa or doing something more hands-on?

Early on, I realized it's not really efficient for me to move to Africa and try to do things on my own. If I were in the field of medicine, like a nurse or a doctor, it would make sense for me to go because that type of help is needed there. But I had a lot of confidence in World Vision, and I loved their model, so the best, most efficient thing I could do was serve alongside an existing organization that was already addressing the needs of people in extreme poverty. They are far more effective then I could be on my own.

What would you say to someone who is winding down their career and looking for their second act?

I definitely think we are all called to do something to make a difference. I know sometimes the transition can be a bit difficult for people, particularly if you've been in the corporate world for a long time, or if you've spent the last twenty or thirty years raising kids, and now they are all out of the house. Change isn't easy, but you have to really look at this season as an opportunity to pursue something that can potentially change the world. Volunteering and giving of your time, talents, and resources, on any level, really helps you get some perspective on life.

Over the course of my life, anytime I took the opportunity to get involved in different charity efforts, it helped me to get outside myself. I think it helped me to be a better player, too. It caused me to be others-centered instead of being self-centered. It gave me a cause to play for. I knew that the better I played, the more money I could donate to various causes. So I would just encourage anyone looking for their second act to start volunteering. See what speaks to your heart.

I always say it doesn't matter what your age is, whether you're a teenager or in retirement, you need to be involved in a cause that's bigger than yourself because that will bring real meaning to your life.

PATTY's POINTS

● **Supporting is as crucial as doing.**

Betsy is a personal friend of mine, and like Betsy, I work with World Vision, so her story resonated with me. I've had similar thoughts regarding how best to support World Vision. As much as I love acting, traveling with World Vision is such a wonderful experience that I could easily see myself doing that full-time. But I can raise awareness and funds as an actress in Los Angeles, and use my platform in the service of bringing clean water and education to millions of people who don't have access to it. That reality actually enriches my career, and makes the trips I can take even more meaningful. But I understand Betsy's desire to spend as much time in Africa as possible.

Maybe you have a similar desire to spend time abroad and be hands-on with humanitarian projects, but you aren't in the right season in your life to be able to do that. Know that your support financially is every bit as crucial as your time. The work cannot get done without funding. If you aren't in a position to give, there are other ways to support: spread the word and help to connect with others who can.

● **Consider your partners.**

I also love how Betsy's friend Debbie was instrumental in helping launch Golf Fore Africa. That kind of support can be crucial to the success of a new project, especially as you are taking a leap into the unknown. To have another person to share the load can ease the worries of starting a new venture. Both Betsy and Debbie made the smart move of looking to others who had already done the heavy lifting to set up their foundation. Why not look around and see who has done a similar thing successfully, and use their expertise to expedite your own process? No need to make it harder than it has to be!

Notice that Betsy connected with someone who already shared her same passion. We've all heard horror stories of people who had bad partners who didn't uphold their end of the deal. Betsy's strategy is one way to safeguard against frustration in the future.

● **Look for ways to give others what you never had.**

It's so admirable that Betsy has also taken on mentoring young women golfers along with her work for Golf Fore Africa. That kind of mentoring wasn't available to her, so Betsy has taken it upon herself to provide it. Often that is the way we find a path to giving back—what wasn't available to us, we give to others.

And this brings up the idea of timing. For many years, Betsy knew she wanted to do something to give back, but she was in a season of learning, growing, and developing her career as a golfer. Sometimes when we have a desire in our hearts, we have to wait for the right time to pursue it. Every experience we have in that waiting period can water and nourish the seed of that desire. Betsy was able to feed that desire in smaller ways as she became a champion golfer. So she kept her dream alive by helping when and where she could. It took years, but now she has come into the fullness of her desire to serve, both with World Vision and with younger golfers. It was worth the wait!

REFLECTION QUESTIONS

1. Where do you see yourself in this story? What part of Betsy's personality, character traits, or journey can you relate to or identify with?

   _____

   _____

   _____

2. What is your greatest takeaway from this story?

   _____

   _____

   _____

3. Earlier in her career, Betsy got involved with volunteer projects in order to take her out of the stress and pressure of her career. Have you tried this strategy? If not, take some time to consider how getting outside yourself can help your perspective on life.

   _____

   _____

   _____

4. Betsy went from developing her talent for her own benefit to using it to benefit others. Can you see a way to use your talent to benefit others?

_____

_____

_____

17

Framing Up Your Second Act

At this point of the book, you are likely in one of two categories of people; either you are ready for your second act, or you're not. Either way, as you read these stories, I hope you learned a little about yourself and broadened your vision for what is possible. I also hope you are feeling a little more inspired, motivated, and encouraged to step out into something new. Or at least to *consider* stepping into something new. (No, a new pair of Jimmy Choos doesn't count.)

So, how do you know if you're ready for your second act? Personally, I think the notion of being "ready" is a little overrated. I mean, there are a lot of things I was never ready for in life that turned out really wonderfully for me. Like becoming a parent. Who is ever ready for that? But even still, there are some telltale signs that it's time to make your move: a sense of restlessness, general dissatisfaction, the awareness that there is more, a dreadful nagging on the inside. Or, very clearly: you feel that you have no other choice. Sounds a little like a midlife crisis, which is another term that has become a bit cliché but signals that you are longing for something more meaningful in your life. The problem with that term is the word *crisis*. A better word would be *metamorphosis*. If you're feeling that restlessness, do your-self a favor: save your cash, skip the Corvette, and forego the face-lift. (Okay, get the face-lift if you want.)

While a metamorphosis sounds much more poetic than a crisis, I never said anything about it being easy. A caterpillar doesn't just waltz into a cocoon one day and then sashay out a beautiful butter-fly the next—it turns into a complete pile of goo in the process. The poor thing doesn't have a clue about what's going on. It's dark and it's lonely, and it's being broken down until it's utterly formless and un-identifiable. Perhaps you can relate? Seasons of transition are seldom easy, but my point here is that you don't have to have a crisis when you are focused on your calling. And if you don't know what your calling is, it's time to find out!

What Moves You?

As we learned from several stories in this book, life gives you clues about what is coming up next. But it's still a good idea to take some time to reflect so you can clearly see what those clues are and figure out how to put them together.

I think understanding your motivations is a good place to start. Now, I'm not a psychologist, but over the course of my life I've paid about as much for therapy as one might pay to get a psychology de-gree, so I feel somewhat justified in sounding like a professional. Plus, I'm an actor. We're paid to get inside people's heads! That said, psy-chologists who actually did go to college will tell you that there are two root motivators in life: pain and pleasure. There is a certain level of motivation that we experience because we want something plea-surable, but there is an even greater level of motivation that drives us when we are striving to avoid something painful—or in some cases, trying to help others avoid something painful.

Our greatest motivation strikes when the pain of staying the same becomes stronger than the pain of change. So stop and think for a moment about your life and how would you feel if nothing changed for the next five years. What about the next ten years . . . or the next twenty? Imagine that it's thirty years from now, and you are doing exactly what you are doing today, day in and day out, having no greater and no less impact on the world. How does the thought of that make you feel? I'm going to leave that right there and let you think more about it later, but do finish this book first.

The other interesting thing about motivation is that you can fuel it by your actions. For example, you may wake up one day and not feel like going to the gym. (Or every day, for some people—okay, for me.) But you make the decision to get dressed, put on your sneakers, drive to the gym, and get on a treadmill. Fine, you stopped to get a latte. At any rate, about ten minutes in, your heart rate is climbing, beads of perspiration are forming, your endorphins kick in, and all of a sudden you are motivated to give it your best! So while it's good to have some awareness about what drives you, know that your *actions* will ultimately fuel your drive. We can't solely rely on our "want to" because we have to decide to keep going on the days when our "want to" isn't there. Which brings me to my next point: just take action because action fuels momentum.

You might be thinking, *But I don't know what to do!* Well, I'm glad you brought that up, because one surefire way to help you learn about yourself and what drives you is to spend sometime volunteering. Betsy and Rachel both had great revelations about their lives through volunteerism. And one thing I've learned from my good friend David Levinson is that there is always a place to volunteer!

David Levinson is the founder of an organization called Big Sunday. Big Sunday organizes volunteers and events to support nonprofits in Los Angeles and the surrounding area. David is an accomplished screenwriter, but found he needed something that was more fulfilling than waiting to find out if his screenplay was going to be produced. He started by volunteering at his temple, and eventually shepherded one weekend of volunteering into a great organization that now operates year 'round. Every year, Big Sunday organizes over two thousand ways for more than fifty thousand people to get involved in the community, from service projects, to materials collection, school beautification projects, and more. It's a wonderful organization that blurs the dividing lines we see in so many other areas of our culture. With Big Sunday, we are all just working together to help our fellow man.

I first heard about Big Sunday from Monica Rosenthal, who memorably played Amy on *Everybody Loves Raymond*. The word *mitzvah* was new to me, but not the concept—a good deed. It was fun to participate in an event that served the community and it really brought the city together. You could volunteer for all kinds of stuff and meet many terrific, interesting, and kindhearted people.

When my kids were growing up, all of their schools required a certain number of community service hours each year, and my boys would inevitably wait until the last minute to tell me they were five or ten hours short—twenty-four hours before the deadline. I would inevitably turn to David: "Hey, David, got anything my fifteen-year-old can do for five hours this weekend?"

"What does he like?"

"Animals are good . . ."

"How about a basset hound rescue in Acton?"

"We're in!"

David would not only save my kids' lives (well, maybe just make sure they graduated to the next grade), but he regularly helps many others in LA—both the recipients and the volunteers.

David will be the first to tell you that deep down inside, everyone wants to help and everybody wants to find a way to give back. Sometimes the challenge is just figuring out how to do it. For some, it's obvious. For people who are painters, or gardeners, or electricians, it's clear when they show up to a school improvement project what they should be doing. Some people's greatest talent is that they are super friendly, and they can walk into a room and make a person feel good. Some people have a talent to do data entry, and there are places for people to volunteer who have that gift, too. Others have a talent to write a check, and those people are needed to make it all happen.

But the best way to explore volunteerism is to do what you enjoy doing. There are so many opportunities. If you aren't comfortable working with homeless people on the street, don't do that. Go help decorate for the holidays at the veterans' home or bake cookies for a nursing home. David is the poster child for volunteerism and he has literally not met a single person who he has not tapped to do something. He told me about the time his own sister got off the plane to come see him. He gave her a big hug and said, "Come with me, we're going to a shelter, and I need you to cut some carrots!" How would it affect all of our families if we volunteered together?

As an organization, Big Sunday really prides itself on the fact that they bring people together from all walks of life and everyone is treated and valued the same, whether you're a homeless person or a movie star. They blur the lines between givers and receivers. They mix it all up because we all have to look after one another. As David frequently says, "No matter who you are, no matter what you do, there's someone who could use your help." And I agree. After all, we are in this thing called life together.

Another great way to learn about yourself and your internal drivers and motivators is by taking personality inventories such as the Enneagram, StrengthsFinder (now known as the CliftonStrengths 34 assessment), and the Myers-Briggs Type Indicator. Remember how Dr. Paul shared that not only did these self-evaluations help him understand himself better, but they helped him understand his wife better, too? Anything that can help our relationships become stronger will help strengthen us during a season of transition.

Make Peace with Your Past

Doing selfwork is so important, and as Dave Dahl reminds us, we are always a work in progress. We can't ever have the attitude that we have arrived because we process in layers, as Sarah Foley has demonstrated in her journey. When moving into a new season, it's a good idea to take some time to reflect and make peace with your past, and take the time to really mourn it if necessary. You have to allow yourself to mourn the person you used to be and acknowledge disappointments, missed opportunities, expectations not met. Then choose to forgive yourself and anyone else who comes to mind in the process.

There are all kinds of ways to symbolically let go of the past. Sarah talked about writing a eulogy and having an actual funeral to let go of the person she used to be. Another way to visualize a release is to write down what you want to let go of on a helium balloon or sky lantern, and then have a moment to let those things fly away. (Use an environmentally safe balloon, of course.) Again, the way you process is personal to you, and as I have said before, if you need a professional to help you, go for it. As Miriam so eloquently demonstrated, when we let go of what didn't work out, and let go of our preconceived ideas and expectations, we make room inside for other things—healthy things, like dreams for the future. Think about what happens when you move into a new home. At some point, during that season of transition, you take time to clean out the clutter in your closets and drawers and get rid of what doesn't serve you—same thing.

I'm a big fan of decluttering. My good friend Tracy McCubbin, author of *Making Space, Clutter Free,* is a professional organizer from whom I've learned a lot. Somehow she is always able to show me how to let go of things I've held on to for years. If I actually follow her advice, in no time at all I don't even remember what it was I was holding on to in the first place. One cool thing Tracy and I have in common is that our birthdays are both on March fourth. "March fourth" is the only date in the calendar that's a command—march forth! Both Tracy and I live by that motto. For me, it was sort of cemented in my life after losing my mother at a young age. I had to contend with moving on even though I had lost the most important person in my life. Perhaps for some, a second act can't really happen unless you can evaluate and reconcile or let go of your first act.

For me, there has definitely been some self-reckoning moments along the way. What could I possibly have to reckon with? you might ask. Well, speaking as an actor, when you are young, you dream of all kinds of things you want to do. Movies are usually right at the top. You can tell by watching the seating at the Golden Globes who are the most important people in the room—the movie stars who are always seated front and center. So that's often the goal when you start out in acting. Of course, you're lucky to get any job in the beginning, especially if you started out with little professional training and no connections, like me. So of course, I'm eternally grateful for the opportunities and success that I've been blessed with. And yet . . . here's the thing . . . I'm sixty-two, so my time left on this planet is limited and I've aged out of roles I've always wanted to play, like Juliet, for example. If my current show runs for a while, which is always the goal, I'll be limited time-wise to small projects when I'm on hiatus in between taping seasons. And if I ever want to write that screenplay, I need to start *now*. So I've had to make peace with the fact that Juliet is now and forever out of the question. But you know what? Mrs. Lovett in *Sweeney Todd* is not. So there are upsides—it's all about perspective.

My point is that we all have losses and disappointments in our lives, and we must learn to embrace all of them, and then let them go, in order to make room for the new adventures that await us. A quote from the poet W. H. Auden describes it best:

> *We would rather be ruined than changed,*
> *We would rather die in our dread*
> *Than climb the cross of the moment*
> *And let our illusions die.*

Be ready to honestly evaluate where you are in every area of your life—your relationships, your career, your vision for the future, and if necessary don't be embarrassed to use a therapist or self-help books or some wise counsel from a friend—whatever helps you to get there. Having a vision is important. When decluttering a house, Tracy talks about having a vision for your home so that you can easily see what needs to go in order to achieve that vision. It's the same way for our lives. What is your vision, and what do you need to let go of in order to get there?

Ready (or Not), Set, Launch

When you are finally ready to move forward, there's pretty much only two ways to do it: you can leap or you can plan. Most of the people in this book are leapers. I'm a leaper, even if that leap begins with a baby step. (But I think planning might make things go a little more smoothly. And there's always "Do a little planning but be flexible.") No matter what, sometimes life has this wonderful way of providing unexpected launchpads into our next season. Like the mother eagle who slings her eaglet out of the nest. While junior is plummeting, in sheer panic, just before he crashes, she swoops down and carries him safely back to the nest . . . only to sling him out again. And again. And again. Until all of a sudden he flies. Yes, life is like that mother eagle sometimes, only it rarely ever swoops down to scoop you up and it burns the nest while you're gone. The good news is that you have the capacity to learn to fly more quickly than you probably give yourself credit for.

One very common launchpad for a second act is loss. These transitions are often abrupt and beyond our control, like being slung from the nest. Perhaps you experienced a layoff, or divorce, or the death of a parent or a loved one. Maybe you had an illness. We see this in Ta'u's story, when an injury ended his football career and prompted his second act in opera. We also see this when Dr. Paul lost his father. He had that deep unrest inside for a long time, but he didn't know what to do with it. It took time for the next steps to become clear. If you are in a season of loss in your life right now, if you've experienced tragedy, first of all, I empathize with you and I'm sorry. Second of all, don't view that loss as an end, view it as a launchpad. Like Miriam, life may have given you something you didn't ask for, but I hope that these stories prove that, with support, you can move forward from it and find meaning from it.

Find Your Tribe

Even though it's *your* second act, you can't stage it alone. Not one person in this book accomplished anything by themselves. A core group of friends with common values helps make it easier to navigate the unchartered terrain. I heard a friend put it this way, "Common experiences unite your past, common dreams unite your future, common values pave the way."

We need relationships in order to be our best. We have to be willing to invest time in these relationships and go deeper than just a scroll and a heart on our social media feeds. Don't get me wrong: social media has been a great tool in a lot of ways and I'm all for it. However, it has its limitations. Nothing can replace face-to-face, eye-to-eye connection and conversation. We are wired for it, and we need to make time for it!

I have wonderful friends that I've known for years, and we are all walking through this second act transition together. There is a core group that have known me way before I had any success. The six of us have married, birthed, adopted, struggled, prayed, and laughed together for more than thirty years. We really support one another in our marriages, our families, and our careers. We have quite a bit of history together, including ups and downs. I always know I can turn to them with and for advice.

We've all grown together, and we've all transitioned in one way or another. One of my friends, who has been an actress for many years, has transitioned into screenwriting. She joined a writing class that she enjoys and she's doing quite well. I now send her scripts to critique because she's extremely perceptive.

It can be hard for someone who has identified as an actress for so long to transition into something different. There's always the hope of extending your career just a little longer because you don't really age out of acting, you just age into another character. However, each actor has to decide how much time and effort they are going to invest in their acting career and when it's time to transition into something else, even if it's not their first love. Screenwriting, directing, or producing are great transitions for actors because those careers are organically tied to performing.

Another one of my friends, an artist, was also ready to make a change. She decided to sell all of her art supplies, but she didn't really know what she wanted to do next, so she set aside some time to do some soul-searching. As part of her self-exploration, she took the pilgrimage El Camino de Santiago, or, in English, the walk of St. James. Now, this is more of a bucket list item than it is a second act per se, but it's a journey of self-discovery and reflection, as well as personal and spiritual growth. There are several routes you can take (St. James walked a lot), and they start in France or Portugal and can take any-where from two weeks to over thirty days to walk. Yes, walk. The entire way. Many people come back touting total internal transforma-tions, and my friend was no different. Now, she still hasn't settled on what she wants to do next, but she is more grounded internally and at peace with herself, her faith, and this stage of her life.

I have another actress friend who transitioned into a physical ther-apy modality called the Alexander technique. She's been studying it for a long time for herself and is considering becoming a practitioner, possibly opening her own studio.

And then there's me. I'm very fortunate that I have the job that I have. I'm doing what I love, and my acting career is still my anchor while I step out into other endeavors like humanitarian efforts, or my Patricia Heaton Home line of housewares, or being a producer and au-thor.

What I see in all of my girlfriends during this stage of transition is the willingness to be open and adventurous, which is contagious among our group! So even if you find your circle of friends stepping out in what seems to be completely different ways from you, there is so much value in being around people who are willing to explore new paths and try new things.

Friends can help us grow, but they can also hold us back. It's im-portant to evaluate your relationships regularly and make sure you aren't investing too much time with people who are not adding value to your life. Don't get me wrong, everyone has seasons where they need to lean on their friends, but I'm talking about people who just constantly suck the life out of you. If a relationship is in the way of your personal growth and progress, that is a relationship to evaluate and perhaps place on a lower priority in your life.

Maybe you are someone who doesn't feel connected to a core group. Maybe you've moved a lot, or had a job transfer, or simply looked up one day and found that the circle you once ran with moved on to different places and seasons. It happens. But it's really important to reach out and build those types of healthy connections any way you can. When I first moved to LA, I found a church to attend because I knew that would help me find community. Betsy found community in her sports fellowship group, which offered emotional and spiritual support. Need I mention that volunteering is another way to make meaningful connections? The important thing is that you reach out and find your tribe!

Again, there's no right or wrong way to frame up your second act. Start from a place of openness and curiosity and step out. You are the architect of your life and every tool you need to design and build your future is already on the inside of you!

Growth in the Second Act

Everything in nature is constantly growing—even the universe is ever-expanding. We, too, should keep growing—intellectually, emotionally, spiritually—long after we start to call ourselves "grown-ups." At the same time, there are seasons to our lives. We need the quiet, dormant seasons to prepare us for new growth ahead. With second acts, as we've seen in this book, a person often goes through a "winter season" in their life right before a transition.

Growth doesn't happen standing still. Growth happens when you challenge yourself and intentionally put yourself in situations that aren't familiar to you. That requires fortitude. No matter how seemingly insignificant, new experiences build that "muscle" of fortitude and develop your confidence so you can step out in bigger ways down the road. This means trying something new even if you think you may not be good at it. You have to be open to failing because it's part of the growing process. Failure isn't the opposite of success—it's part of it!

The Art of Growth

When you step out of your comfort zone, you are open to new experiences, new people, and new opportunities, even if you can't see exactly where those opportunities will lead.

Not long ago, a friend called and asked if I would join her for a three-day art class. I loved to draw when I was little and I have a bit of an artistic flair—but not enough to build a career on. I wasn't sure I really wanted to go to this art class. I was worried I'd be bad. And I was worried I had fallen into a cliché: women get to a certain point in life and they start basket weaving or sculpting or . . . taking art classes. And I was slightly worried about the commitment. A three-day, six-hour-a-day art class? Seemed a little intense. But after I thought about it for a minute, I decided to go. I knew it would be fun to try something new and spend some time with my friend. It was a still life class with oils. I mean, how bad could it possibly be? How bad could *I* possibly be?

As it turns out, pretty bad. When the first day of the class arrived, I really had no idea what to expect. I was feeling a little self-conscious—a brand-new experience, only my one friend for support—but I assured myself it wasn't rocket science. I walked into the room and could tell immediately that I was in completely over my head. I was running a bit late, so when I arrived everyone had already started on their canvases, and I could see these women (yes, it was all women) were accomplished painters. The instructor was a serious Dutch gal who had studied painting in Florence and currently ran a studio in New York. This was not paint by numbers. There was no sipping wine, no joking about our husbands, no tipsily complimenting each other's work. No, this class was actually about improving your painting skills, and I wasn't sure I had any. As one would expect, the instructor's paintings were incredible, but so were everyone else's. Even if they weren't artists for a living, some of them probably could be. I just thought, *What in the world am I doing here?* I really wanted to sneak out the back, but the class was fairly small and when you're me, it's not so easy to sneak out of anywhere. I sucked it up and stayed the entire six-hour day, all the while thinking how out of place I felt.

I really didn't want to go back. At the same time, I didn't want to disappoint my friend and I hate admitting defeat. (Also, the class was expensive—that should have been my first clue—and I didn't want to waste my money.) So, the next day I woke up, gave myself a pep talk, and made myself go back. The second day, I walked in and looked at all the other canvases and thought, *I'm so far behind all of these people.* But I had already decided that I would press on and find a way to have a good time anyway.

By the end of the third day, miraculously I was still alive. The instructor did comment on what a sloppy painter I was (I managed to get paint on my clothes and my face), but she was impressed with my work, given that this was my first painting class. And I found out that I actually wasn't too bad! Or maybe the teacher was just that good. Either way, my point here is that if I never pick up a paintbrush again, just pushing past that fear and making myself get out of my comfort zone was useful to me. The experience didn't kill me; in fact, it caused me to grow. No one went online afterward and said, "Patricia Heaton is an atrocious artist, and everyone needs to know this." No, it was simply a couple of days of painting with some really talented women. And I got to spend some quality time with my friend, too.

Once I finally stopped comparing myself to others and stopped worrying about what they would think of my painting, I enjoyed focusing on something new for those three days. When you singularly focus on something like painting, playing piano, or learning a new language, you give your mind a break from all the things regularly spinning around in there. That's the great benefit to finding a hobby and taking some time for yourself.

That's why I love golf. After *Everybody Loves Raymond* finished, I had time to play again (and golf takes a *lot* of time). Then *The Middle* came along and the twelve-hour days left me with time only for my family. Once *The Middle* ended, I once again attempted to get back on the links. It was going pretty well until *Carol's Second Act* came along, and I've had less time to play. I try to keep a hand in it as often as I can because, just like painting, it helps me give my mind a break. It's also great for meeting new people. And it's such a challenging game that it tests your patience and commitment, all things I need to work on. And just like in that painting class, you have to work hard to let go of your ego.

One weekend, I decided to take a women's golf clinic at a local club. When I signed up, I had no idea who was going to be there. I just assumed I wasn't going to know anybody, which was hard because while I'm a better golfer than I am a painter, I'm really not a very good golfer. I had to be okay with being terrible in front of people I didn't know but who probably knew me.

However, as I was driving to the clinic that morning, I found myself to be surprisingly optimistic about it all. Normally, I would be thinking, *Oh, I haven't played in so long, I know I'm going to be awful. They are probably going to stick me in a foursome, and I'll be the worst one, and the other people will be upset that they have this terrible golfer with them, and I'll be so embarrassed*, and so on. But I changed my perspective after that art class. I wasn't worried. I was actually excited. I thought, *I wonder who I will meet today. I wonder what kind of adventure I'll experience. I wonder how much I can actually improve my game.* Honestly, it felt a little strange because I tend to be slightly pessimistic. I always prepare myself for the worst-case scenario, especially in new situations—where there are a lot of unknowns. But that morning, I was different. I was hopeful. I was looking forward to learning new things and meeting new people. Most of all, I expected to simply have a good time.

I was surprised by my own optimism. We actors often expect to fail miserably in front of people. Most actors are insecure, no matter what level of success we achieve. The thoughts that go through an actor's mind before he/she steps onto a set or stage: *I'm awful! Why did they hire me? Why did I say yes? I can't act! I won't remember my lines! Okay, that's my cue!* I recently heard Sir Anthony Hopkins say that he is very insecure—which is comforting to know! An actor of his stature and accomplishment feels the same way as I do! So the optimism that bubbled up on my way to the golf course was a surprise—a pleasant surprise. If only I could face every day with that kind of openness.

On the green, I was greeted by a number of women I knew. I saw old friends and met many new ones. We ended up having a wonderful time. I found a great group of ladies to go golfing with who don't mind that I'm a beginner (after twenty years of trying).

I think if we can push ourselves out of our comfort zones in little ways like this, it helps us build up confidence to step out when bigger opportunities come along—such as a career change, a move, or another type of second act adventure. When you change your self-talk, when you stop worrying about being judged, you realize that most people actually want to help you grow.

I know, it's tough. But we all have that nagging inner voice that says, *You're going to be terrible and people are going to judge you and not want you on their team.* When you hear that voice, you have to stop for a moment, acknowledge those thoughts, then put them aside. You have to decide to tune out that voice and tune in to the voice of optimism, the voice that says, *I am capable, I am likable, and I'm going to have a great time learning something new!* (I realize I sound like the Al Franken character Stuart Smalley and his daily affirmations: "I'm good enough, I'm smart enough, and, doggone it, people like me!" But what he's saying is true!) One thing to remember about insecurity is that everyone has it about something (even Sir Anthony!).

There is an element of narcissism to our insecurity. We think everyone is looking at us and thinking about us and judging us. That's a bit self-important, isn't it? The fact is, most everyone is thinking about themselves! Of course, there are those who are judgmental, so be prepared. But you don't want those folks in your life anyway, so ignore them (but pray for them, too—people like that are usually in pain). Most people who desire to grow, or learn, or improve a skill also want to help others grow and learn and improve, too. You may have to get out there and find those people. My husband had to do just that. Years ago, when he told his friends that he wanted to come to America to become an actor, they scoffed at him. But when he arrived in New York, he had a completely different experience. Everywhere he went, he found people who encouraged him, whether it was a lead on an apartment for rent or a recommendation for an acting teacher.

What to Do Next

As crazy as it sounds, when you aren't really certain what to do next . . .
Just. Go. Do. Something. At this point, I could drop the mic and end
the book, but with a history of getting four boys out the door and to
school every day for twenty-five years, my motherly instincts won't let
me send you off without making sure your backpack is zipped up with
some options for your journey.

- Volunteer: If I haven't made it super clear that volunteering
  is an excellent way to learn about yourself, explore your passions, and find a bridge to your second act, let me just say it
  one more time. (Wow, I really do sound like a mom.) Where can
  you volunteer? Check out the local Boys & Girls Clubs, Habitat
  for Humanity, a local food bank, or simply search "places to
  volunteer near me." If you are part of a church, that's a great
  place to get started, too!

- Take a Class: Remember, taking a class in an area that interests
  you doesn't mean it has to be the end all, be all of what you
  end up doing. Just stepping out and learning something new
  will do wonders for you. Also, many state colleges offer free
  tuition to adults age sixty-two-plus, so look online for options
  in your area. And speaking of online, there are many online
  learning options as well. An in-person class is good for net-
  working and building community, but if all you have is the
  internet, there's a lot to learn! If you want to take a class geared
  specifically toward exploring a second act career, Marci Albo-
  her, vice president of Encore.org, has a free class on LinkedIn
  Learning. She also has a wonderful book called *The Encore Career Handbook* that you may find useful.

- Read Books: And speaking of books, keep reading! Of course,
  I probably don't need to tell you that since you made it to the
  end of this book. Reading is a wonderful way to expand the
  mind, find inspiration, learn, and grow. So keep up the good
  reads!

- Listen to Podcasts: Need inspiration on the go? Podcasts are a wonderful way to feed your mind and expand your horizons. Listen while you are getting ready, working out, driving, or even cooking dinner. Nowadays, we have access to so many wonderful leaders and motivational speakers.
- Journal: Journals don't have to be just about your deepest emotions and private thoughts. You can write a gratitude journal and list things daily that you are thankful for. You can write goals, you can write inspiring thoughts, whatever you'd like. Journaling helps you slow down and really connect with your inner drive and motivation. At least that's what they tell me. Okay, I'm putting this on my to-do list, too!
- Travel: Travel is a wonderful way to stimulate your mind and expand your outlook. Travel doesn't have to be expensive to be mentally expansive. A one-day road trip to explore a neighboring city can be enough to give you a healthy change of scenery and allow you to step outside your familiar territory. Remember, start with baby steps if you have to. If it's in your budget, make it a weekend trip. Be spontaneous! Don't just dream of getting out of Dodge, make a plan and make it happen. Too often life slips by and we are left with coulda, woulda, shoulda. Don't "shoulda" all over yourself! Now is your time!

They say all good things must come to an end, and here we are. I hope you've enjoyed these stories and that you've found hope and encouragement for your second act, a new or renewed sense of purpose, and a lot of inspiration and ideas! If you've been struggling, or feeling directionless or bored, or just thinking about making a change, I hope I've given you the kick start you need to step out, try something new, and make some changes.

Before you close this book, I want to encourage you to go back and read through your answers to the reflection questions. Find three things you can commit to do today to get going in the right direction. I mean it! Don't let another day slip by without taking a step. And why not grab your friends and make a "second act" party out of it? Gather your besties and have a free-range inspiration session—share ideas, make vision boards, write goals, and hold each other accountable! And who knows, you may find someone who'd like to come along for the ride. Someone once said, "Sharing adventures means enjoying them 100 percent more."

Don't forget that the journey isn't just about your destination, but about everything that happens along the way—what you learn, who you meet, and how you change or how you change others. And if you decide you are ready for an adventure, please let me know! Drop me a line on @patriciaheaton on Instagram or Twitter and OfficialPatricia HeatonFanPage on Facebook. I'd love to hear your inspiring story. Who knows how your adventure might spark inspiration for someone else's. For now, let me be the first to officially say . . . welcome to Your Second Act!—aaaaaand ACTION!

DIGGING DEEPER

1. Do you have some new ideas, thoughts, or feeling about yourself or your second act after reading this book? Use the space provided to write about what has changed inside of you. Do you have a new sense of hope or possibility? Do you have a clearer vision for what you'd like to see in your future? Are you nervous, excited, or scared? Remember, all of those feelings are part of getting out of your comfort zone. On the other side of the unknown is adventure, satisfaction, and the wonderful sense of fulfillment.

_____

_____

_____

_____

_____

_____

_____

_____

_____

2. Take some time to freely dream: Oftentimes, we set our focus on the limits we see in our lives instead of the possibility. Sometimes, a simple shift in focus is all we need to see an open door of opportunity. Take the limits off your dreams first—if you could do anything or go anywhere, if you had all the connections and resources you needed, what would you do? Where would you go? How would you use your influence to impact the world around you?

3. Take some time and consider what you wrote on the previous pages. Did you write anything that surprised you or something you haven't considered before? While you may not be able to do all of the things you listed, by allowing yourself to freely dream, you have clues about the direction your heart is telling you to go. What are some "baby steps" you could take in the direction of those desires? Like Ta'u, you can learn by studying people who are doing what you desire to do. Like Larry and Sara, you can start with one dish, before you can open a restaurant. Like Rachel, you can collect a box of clothes for the needy before you open a storefront. List as many ideas or "baby steps" you can think of that may be related to your desires and dreams.

_____

_____

_____

_____

_____

_____

_____

_____

_____

_____

_____

_____

_____

ACKNOWLEDGMENTS

My sincere gratitude goes to the following individuals who contributed to the success of this project and helped keep me closer to the line of sanity as a result:

Adam Griffin & Ryan Bundra
project management

Joanna K. Hunt
research, writing, and collaboration
www. joannakhunt.com

CeCe Yorke
True Public Relations

Joe Magnani and Jared Schlachet
cover photo

Kathleen Lynch, Jackie Seow, and Lewelin Polanco
cover and layout design

And a very special thanks to Jonathan Karp, Emily Graff, and the entire team at Simon & Schuster.

NOTES

2   **one step short of crazy:** Singyin Lee, "10 Things You Should Know About Passion (And How to Find Yours)," Hongkiat.com, May 23, 2019, https://www.hongkiat.com/blog/finding-passion/.

27   **touted by the Food Network:** Natalie B. Compton, "Golden State Grub: The Best Things to Eat in California," Foodnetwork .com, https://www.foodnetwork.com/restaurants/packages/best -food-in-america/photos/what-to-eat-in-california.

64   **no downside to practicing more gratitude:** Lisa Firestone, "The Healing Power of Gratitude," *Psychology Today*, November 19, 2015, https://www.psychologytoday.com/us/blog/compassion-matters /201511/the-healing-power-gratitude.

67   **Betsy and Golf Fore Africa granted more than $9.4 million:** "Betsy King," Golfforeafrica.org, http://golfforeafrica.org/dev _site/wp-content/uploads/2018/05/Bio-GFA-Betsy.pdf.

87   **The cost of caring for Americans with autism:** Autism Speaks, "Autism Facts and Figures," Autismspeaks.org, https://www.au tismspeaks.org/autism-facts-and-figures.

107   **engaging with the arts raises your EQ:** Vaibhav P. Birwatkar, "The Art of Emotional Intelligence," Noemalab.eu, https://noema lab.eu/ideas/27417/.

108   **the ability to recognize, evaluate, and regulate your own emotions:** "Emotional Intelligence Test Free-EQ Test Free On- line," Iq-test.net, https://www.iq-test.net/eq-test.html.

157   **a brain disease with no known cure:** Dani Klein Modisett, "Using Humor to Combat Dementia," AARP.org, June 2018,

https://www.aarp.org/caregiving/health/info-2018/humor-alz
heimers-dementia-caregiving.html.

160   **Every sixty-five seconds:** Fish Center for Alzheimer's Research
Foundation, "Alzheimer's Disease Facts and Statistics," Alzinfo
.org https://www.alzinfo.org/understand-alzheimers/alzheimers
-disease-facts-and-statistics/.

206   **Optimists are not simply being Pollyannas:** Hans Villarcia,
"How the Power of Positive Thinking Won Scientific Credibil-
ity," *The Atlantic*, April 23, 2012, https://www.theatlantic
.com/health/archive/2012/04/how-the-power-of-positive-think
ing-won-scientific-credibility/256223/.

227   **you can leap or you can plan:** Marci Albahor, *The Encore Career Handbook: How to Make a Living and a Difference in the Second Half of Life* (New York: Workman, 2013).

ABOUT THE AUTHOR

Patricia Heaton is an Emmy Award–winning actress who has played two iconic moms on the long-running sitcoms *Everybody Loves Raymond* and *The Middle*. In 2001, Heaton cofounded FourBoys Entertainment, a production company that she runs with her husband, David Hunt. They have produced many projects, including the features *Moms' Night Out* and *Amazing Grace*, about the life of abolitionist William Wilberforce. Heaton recently launched her homewares line, Patricia Heaton Home, with Walmart. Born out of her love for spending quality time with family and friends, this beautiful and affordable product line was a natural next step after her Emmy Award–winning Food Network series, *Patricia Heaton Parties*, and her first cookbook, *Patricia Heaton's Food for Family and Friends*. A committed philanthropist, Heaton is the founding member of World Vision's Celebrity Ambassador Network. She lives in Los Angeles with her husband.